T0013393

LENNIE

ADVICE FROM A BLOB

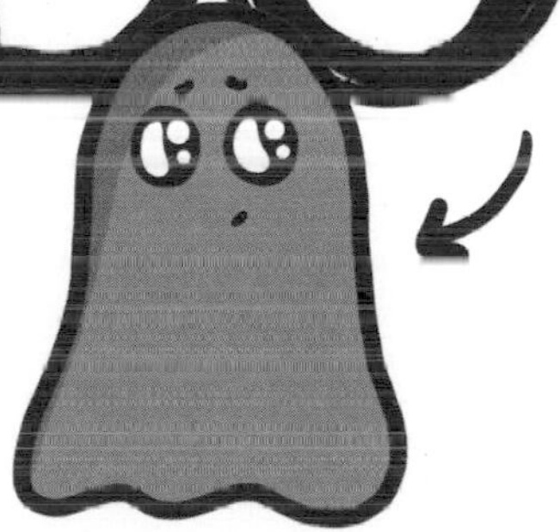

HOW TO FIND PEACE IN THIS MESSY BEAUTIFUL CHAOTIC EXISTENCE

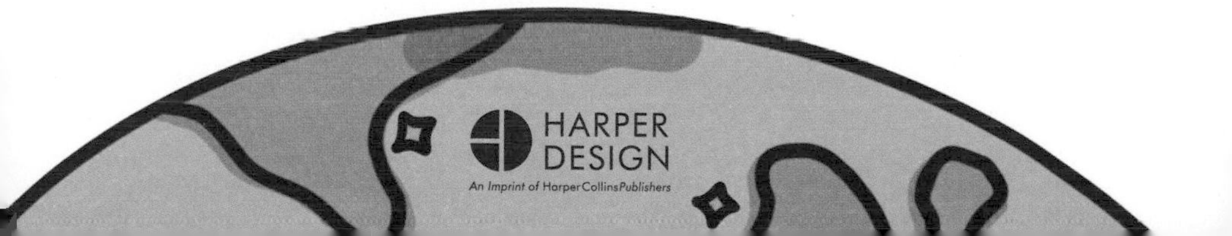

HARPER DESIGN
An Imprint of HarperCollinsPublishers

ADVICE FROM A BLOB.
Text and illustrations copyright © 2023 by It's Lennnie.
All rights reserved. No part of this book may be used or reproduced
in any manner whatsoever without written permission except in
the case of brief quotations embodied in critical articles and reviews.
For information, address HarperCollins Publishers,
195 Broadway, New York, New York 10007.

HarperCollins books may be purchased for educational, business,
or sales promotional use. For information please email
the Special Markets Department at SPsales@harpercollins.com.

Published in 2023 by
Harper Design
An Imprint of HarperCollins*Publishers*
195 Broadway
New York, NY 10007
Tel: (212) 207-7000
Fax: (855) 746-6023
harperdesign@harpercollins.com
www.hc.com

Distributed throughout the world by
HarperCollins Publishers
195 Broadway
New York, NY 10007

ISBN 978-0-06-322251-6

Printed in Thailand

23 24 25 26 27   10 9 8 7 6 5 4 3 2 1

CONTENTS

OH HELLO, HUMAN!
MY NAME'S

lemmie

I'm a little blob that was sent by the book gods to come check on you.

4

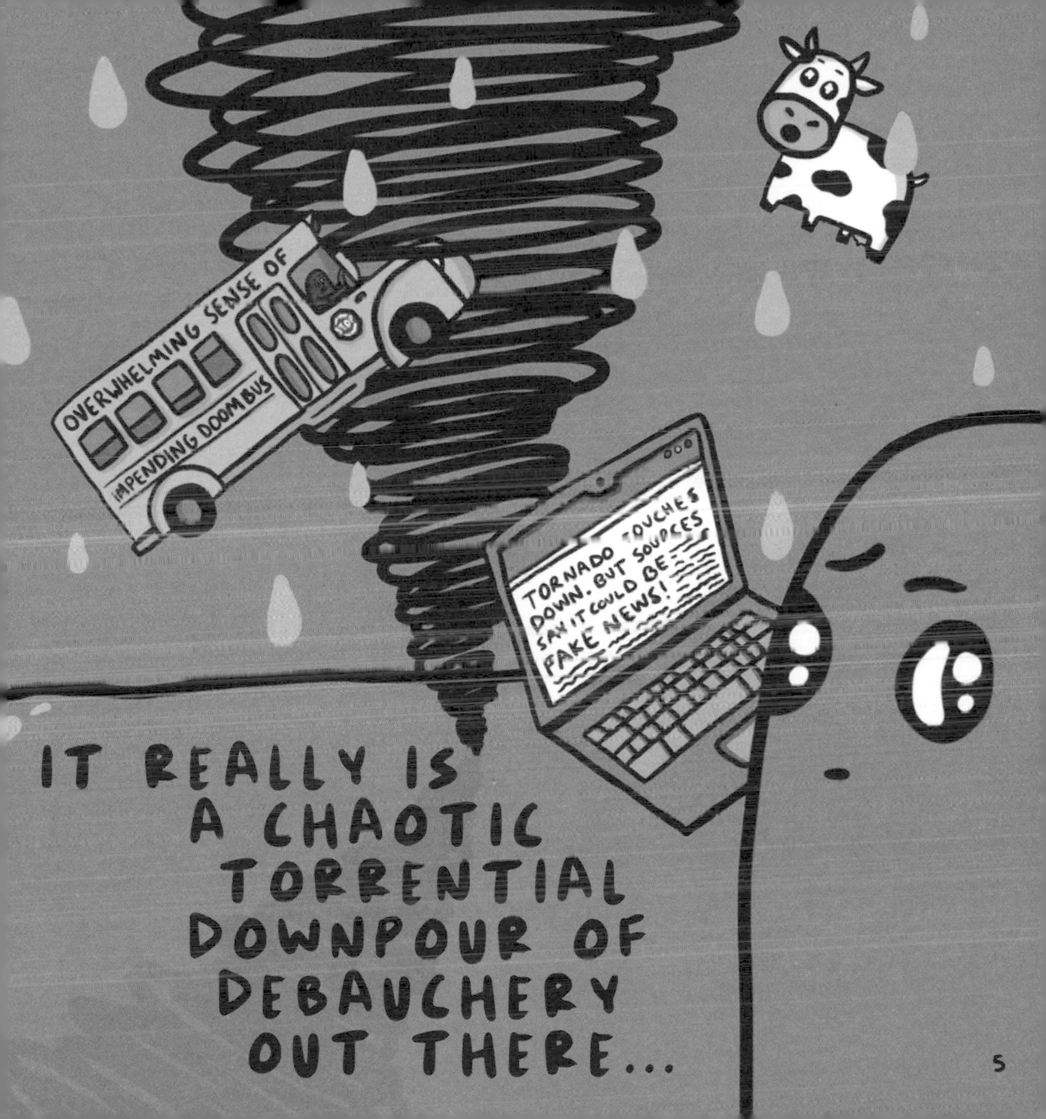
OVERWHELMING SENSE OF
IMPENDING DOOM BUS
TORNADO TOUCHES DOWN. BUT SOURCES SAY IT COULD BE FAKE NEWS!
IT REALLY IS A CHAOTIC TORRENTIAL DOWNPOUR OF DEBAUCHERY OUT THERE...

BUT I **PROMISE** THAT YOU'RE GONNA BE OKAY. ♥

REALLY TRULY ABSOLUTELY POSITIVELY FINE.

... EVEN IF IT DOESN'T FEEL LIKE IT RIGHT NOW.

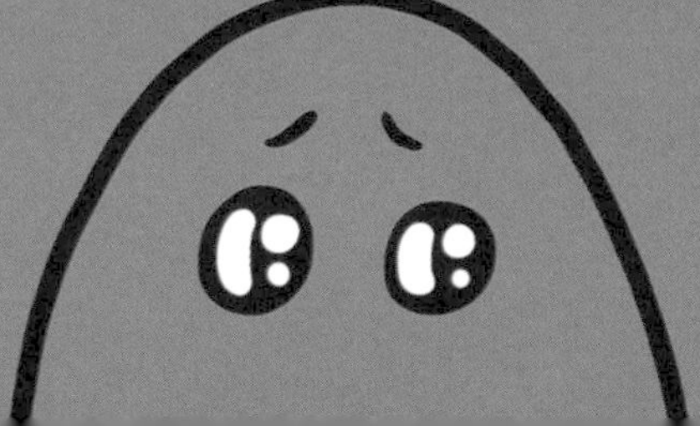

I'M A BLOB SO...
I KNOW THESE THINGS
see below
Official Decree
BLOBS JUST KNOW THINGS.
DON'T QUESTION IT.

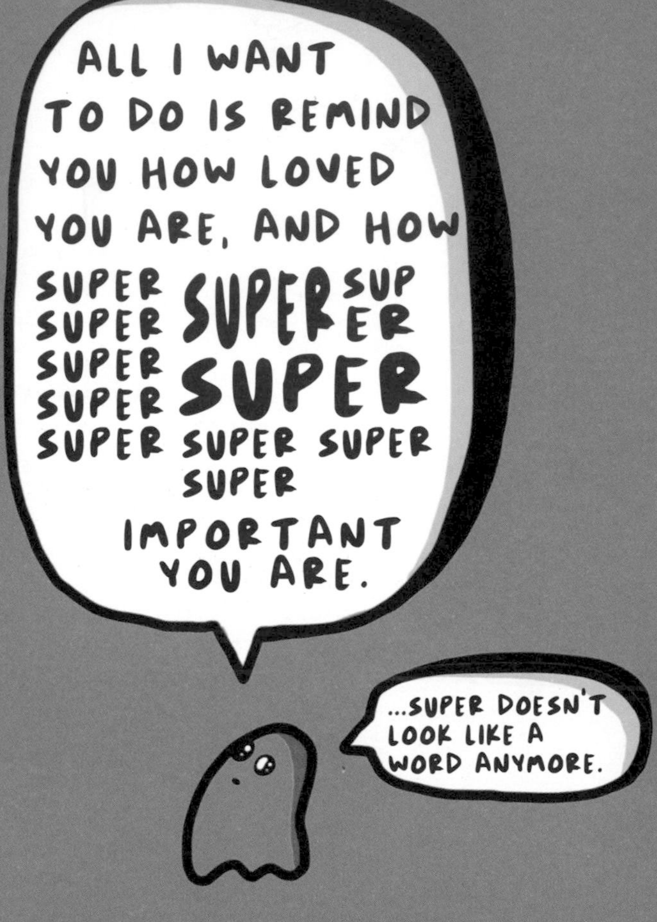
ALL I WANT TO DO IS REMIND YOU HOW LOVED YOU ARE, AND HOW SUPER SUPER SUP ER SUPER SUPER SUPER SUPER SUPER SUPER SUPER SUPER SUPER SUPER IMPORTANT YOU ARE.
...SUPER DOESN'T LOOK LIKE A WORD ANYMORE.

AND THAT'S WHY I MADE THIS BOOK!

9

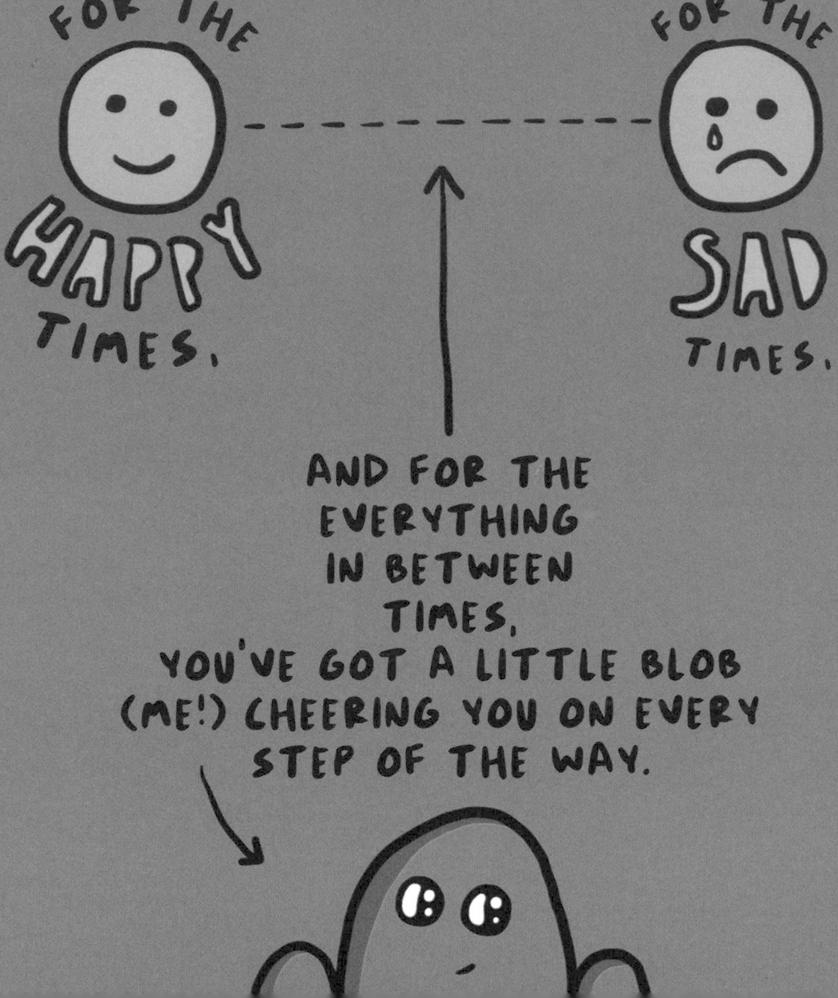
FOR THE HAPPY TIMES.
FOR THE SAD TIMES.
AND FOR THE EVERYTHING IN BETWEEN TIMES,
YOU'VE GOT A LITTLE BLOB (ME!) CHEERING YOU ON EVERY STEP OF THE WAY.

I see you
and I love you.
whole-heartedly
and
unconditionally.

NOW LET'S GET INTO IT,
SHALL WE?!!!

woo!

I

The Feeling

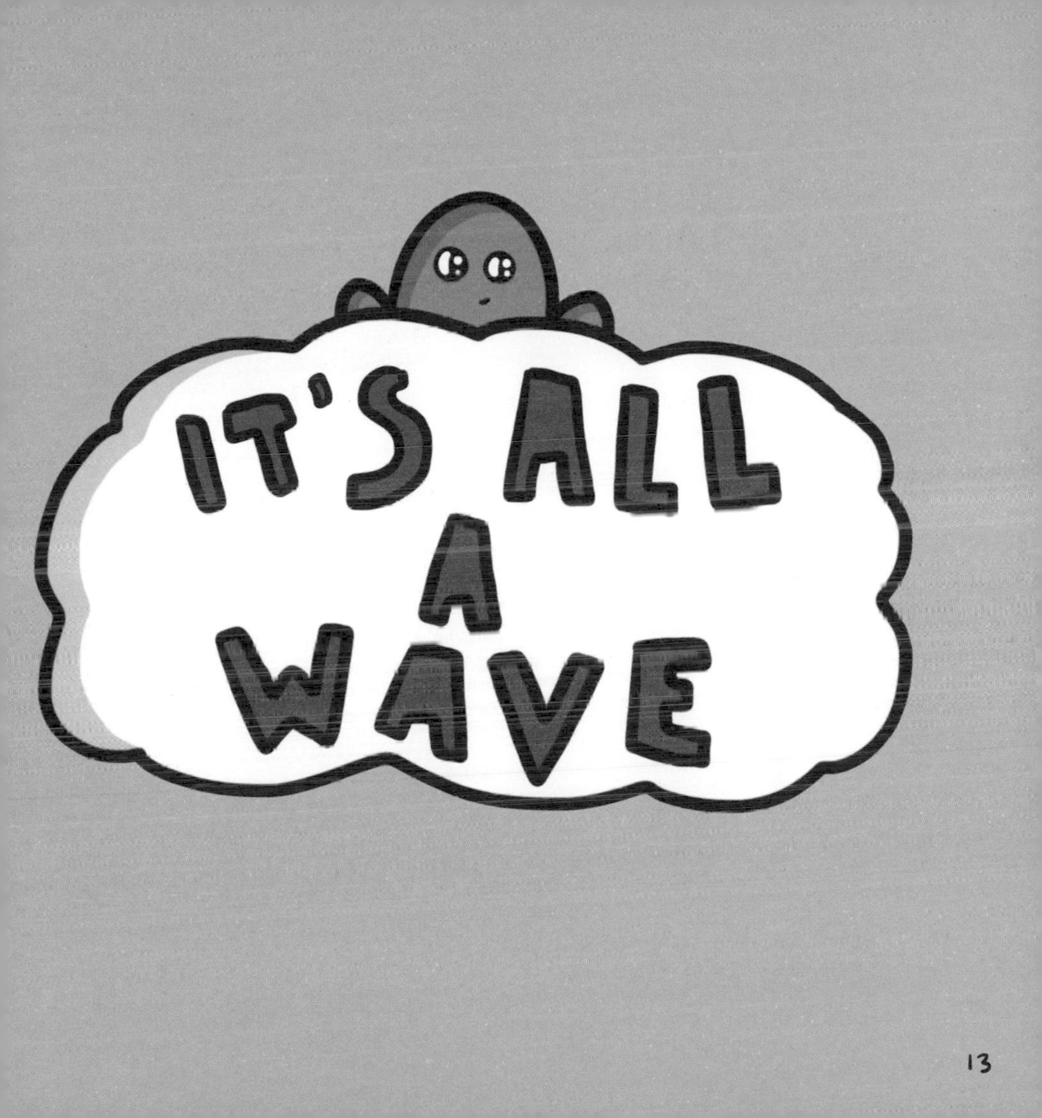
IT'S ALL
A
WAVE

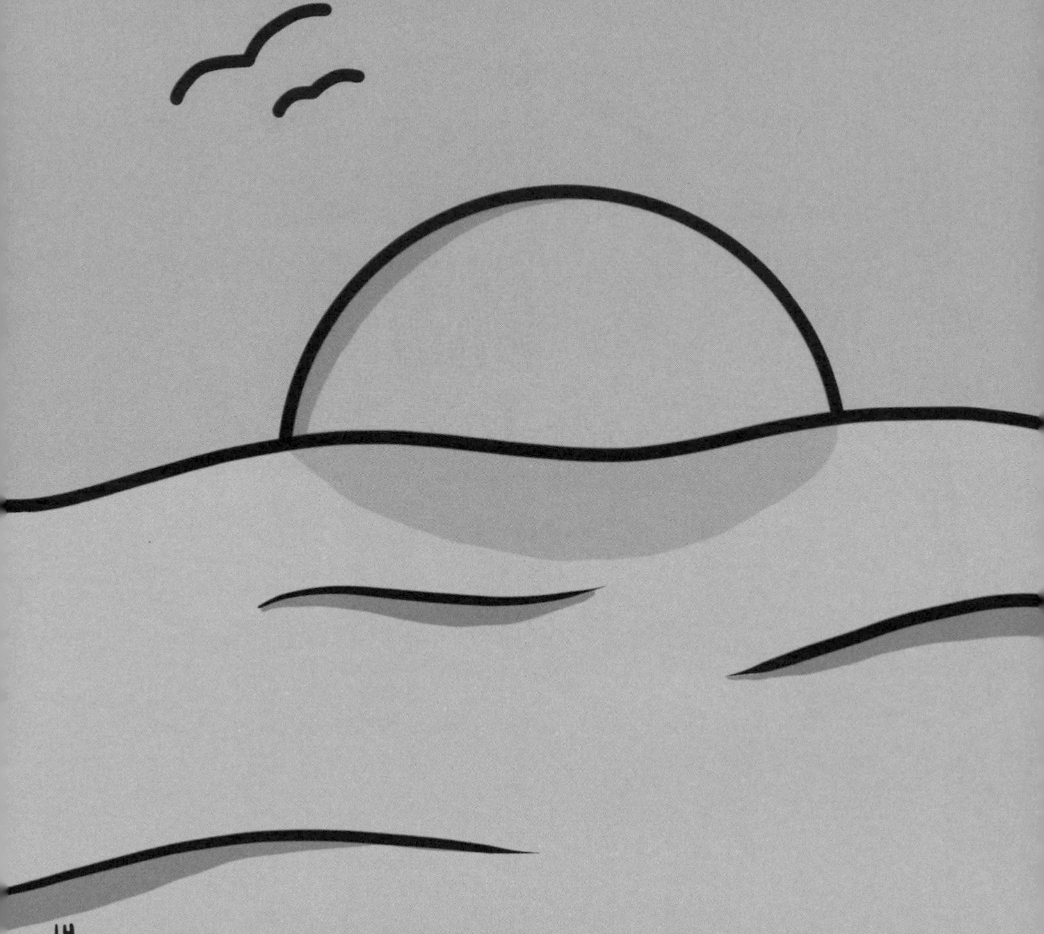

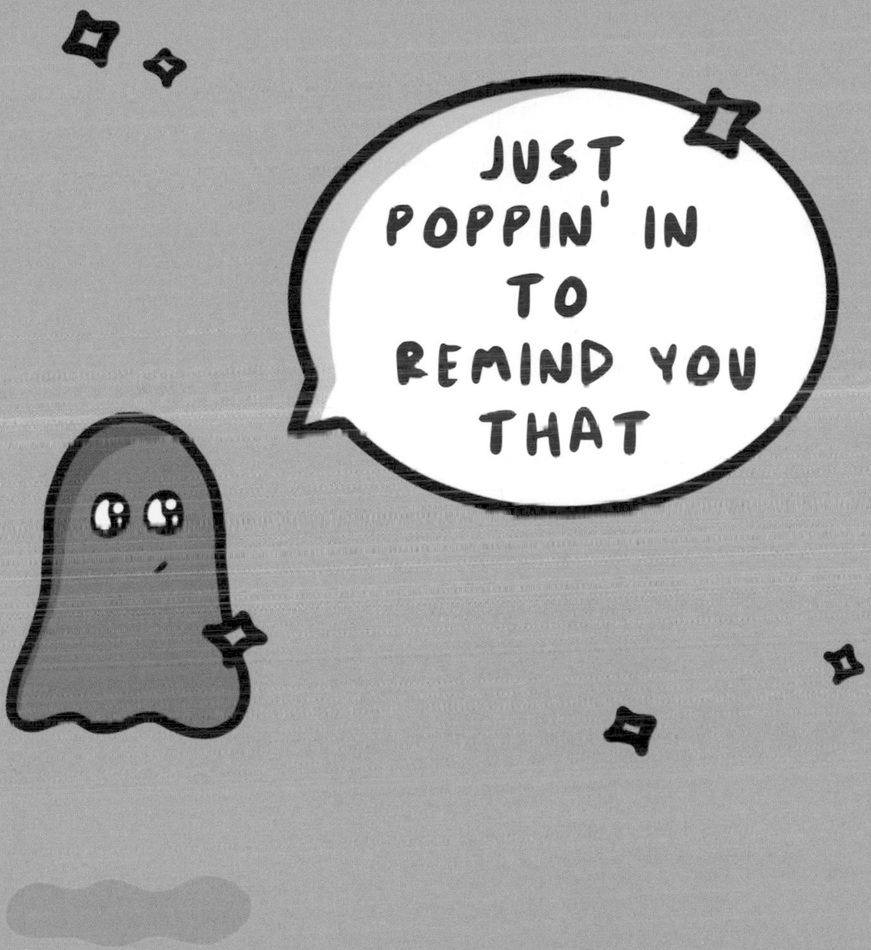
JUST POPPIN' IN TO REMIND YOU THAT

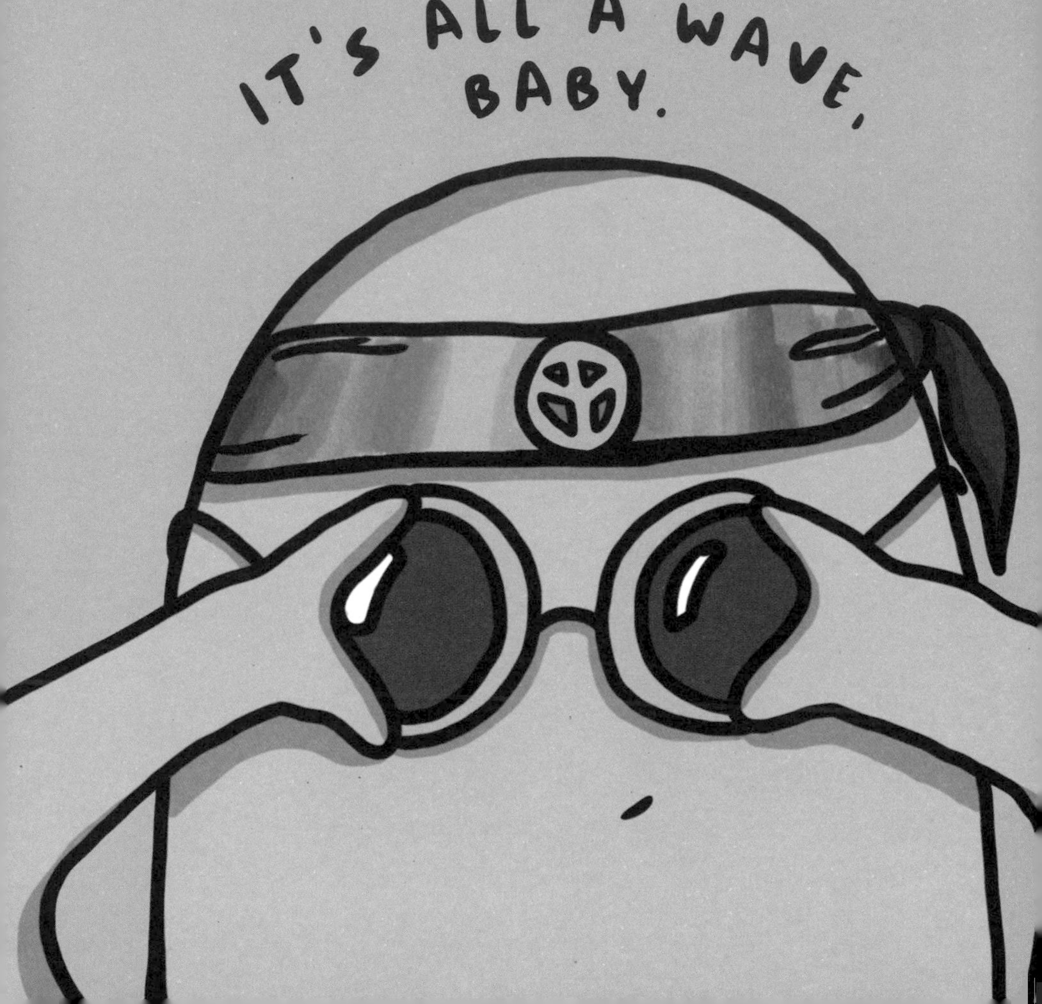
IT'S ALL A WAVE,
BABY.

ONE SECOND
YOU'RE
ON TOP
OF THE ENTIRE
FREAKING OCEAN
FEELING INVINCIBLE.

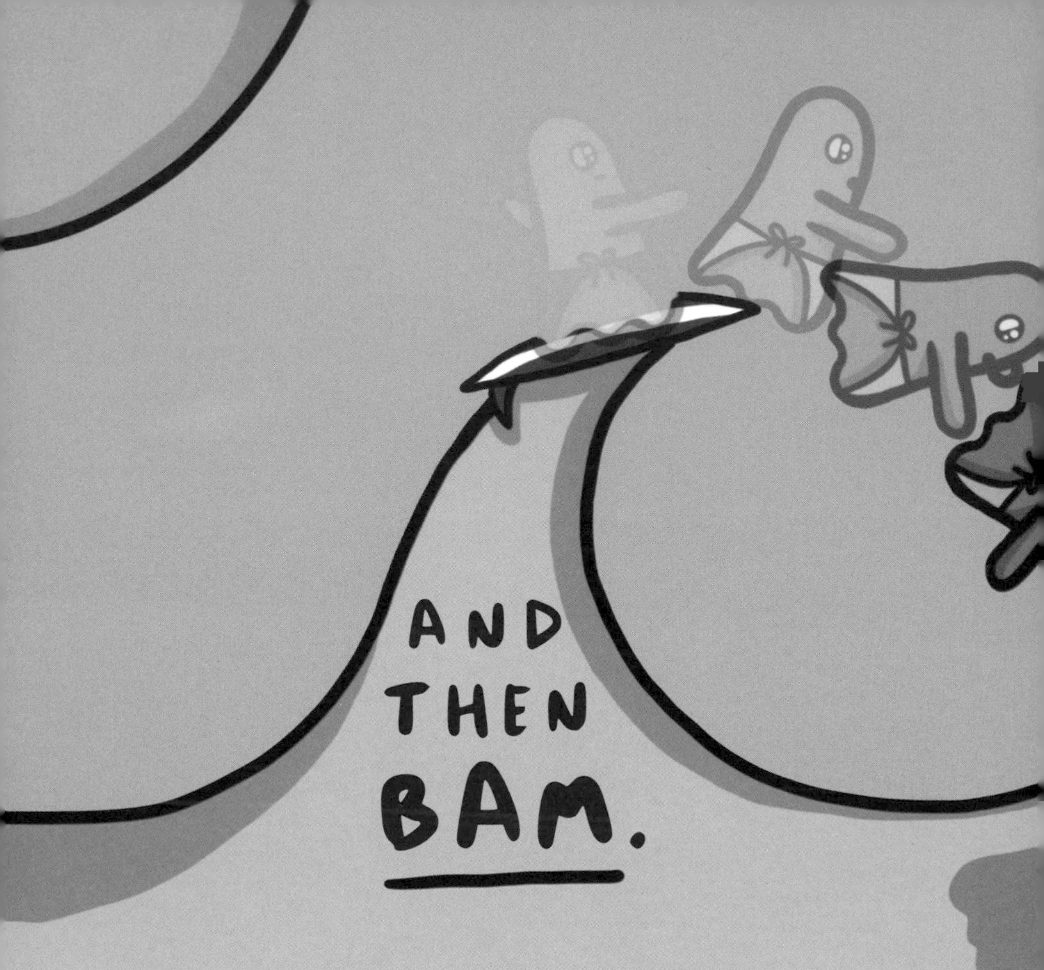

AND THEN **BAM.**

YOU'RE
FACE
FIRST
INTO
ROCK
BOTTOM.

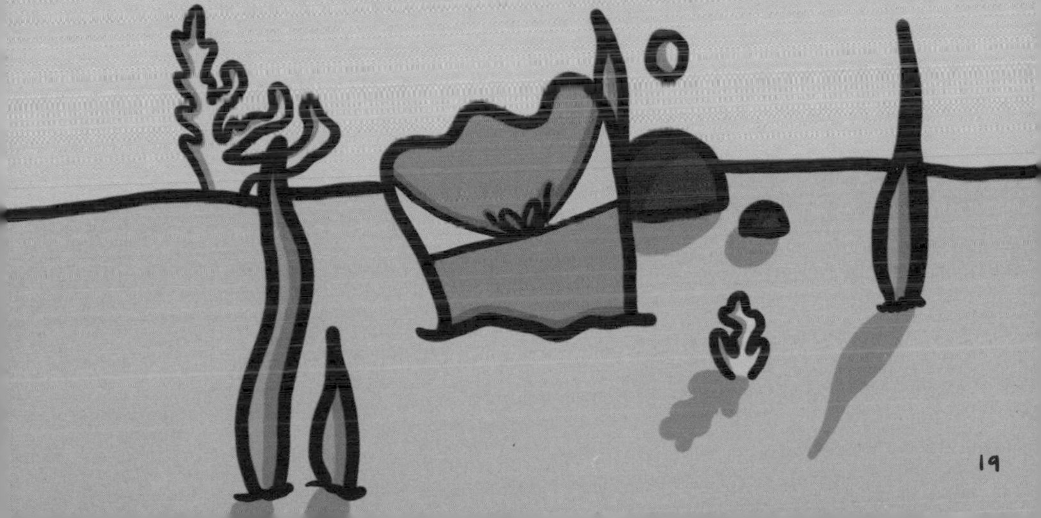

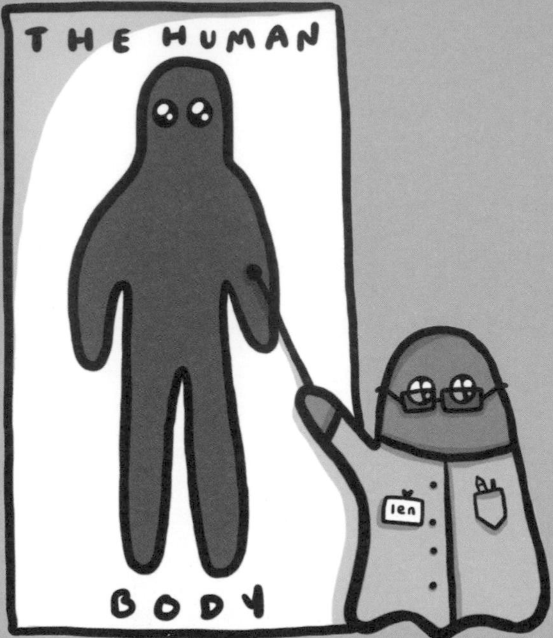
THE HUMAN
BODY
len

BUT YOU KNOW WHAT'S DOPE ABOUT THE SCIENTIFIC MAKEUP OF THE HUMAN BODY?

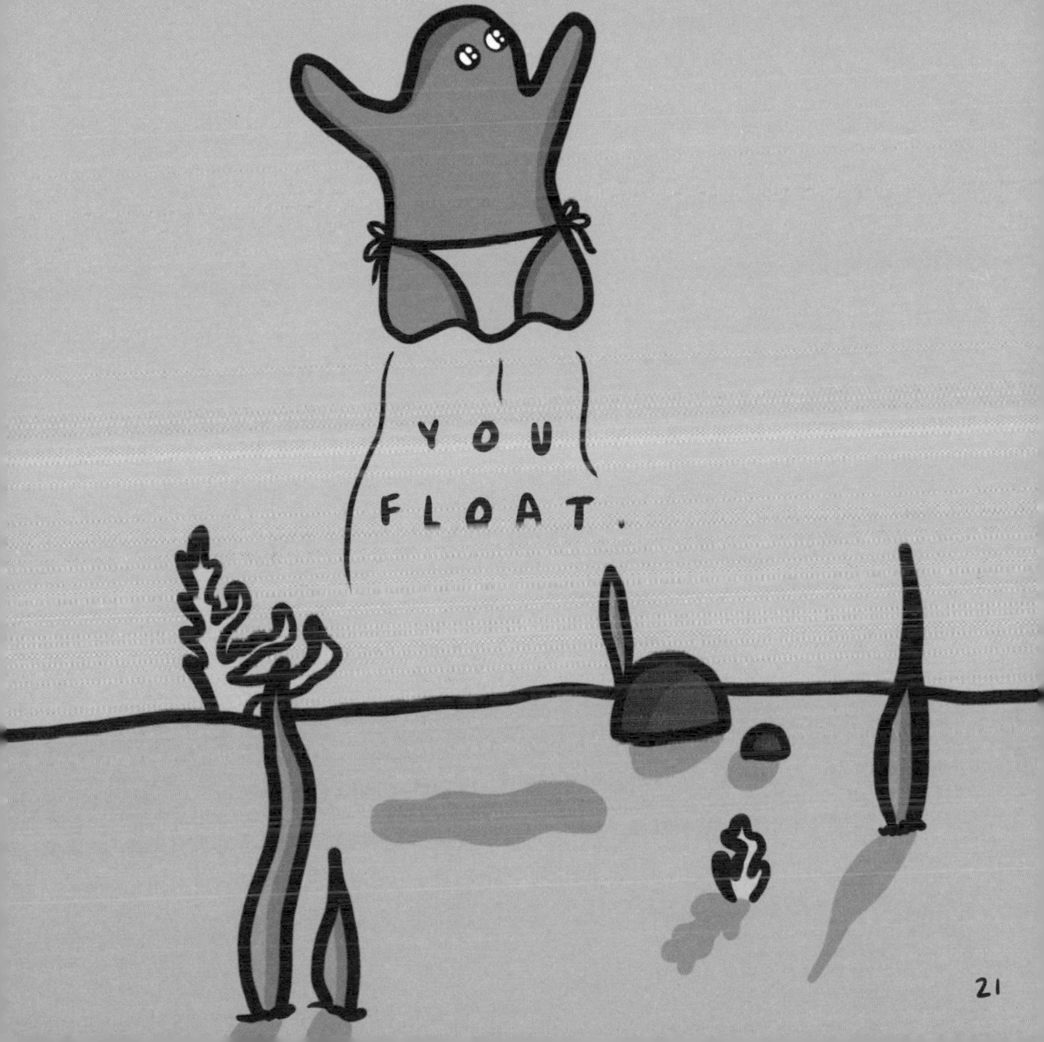
YOU
FLOAT.

YOU FLOAT, AND YOU FLOAT, AND YOU FLOAT, AND YOU FLOAT, BACK UP TO THE SURFACE.

AND THEN YOU WAIT...

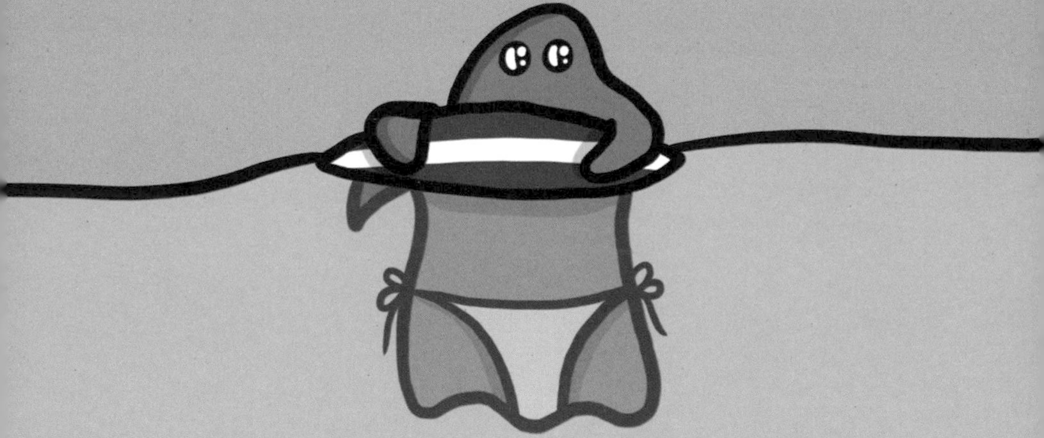

AND

EVENTUALLY,

SOMETIMES EVEN RIGHT WHEN YOU'RE ABOUT TO GIVE UP,

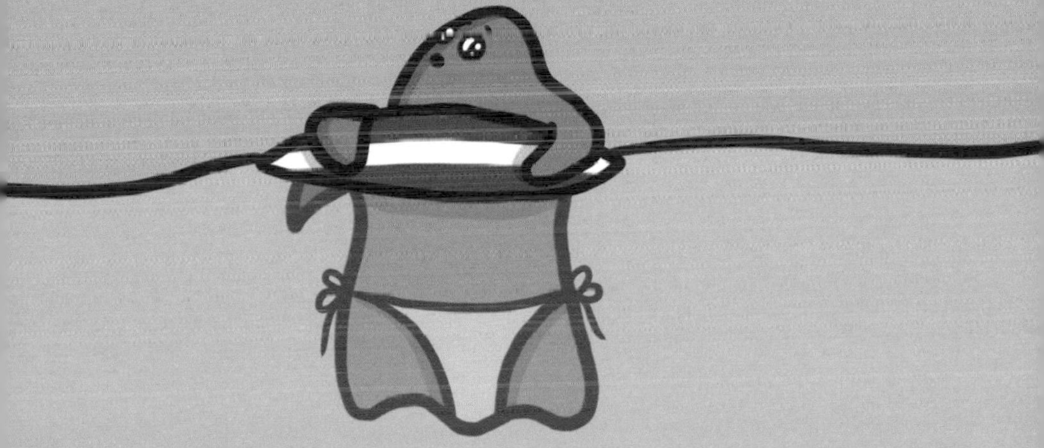

THE BIGGEST, MOST BEAUTIFUL WAVE COMES

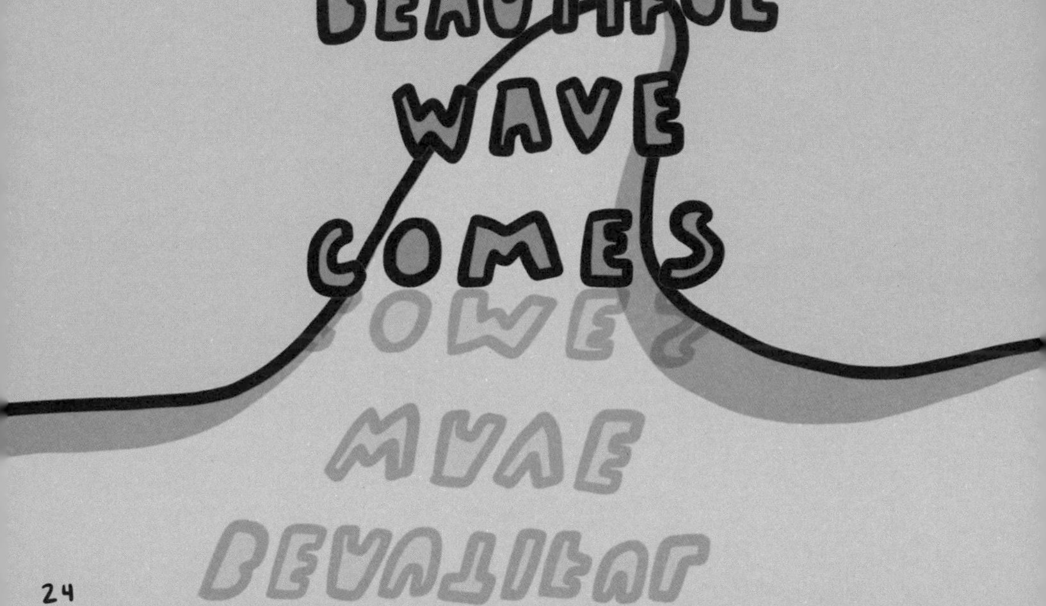

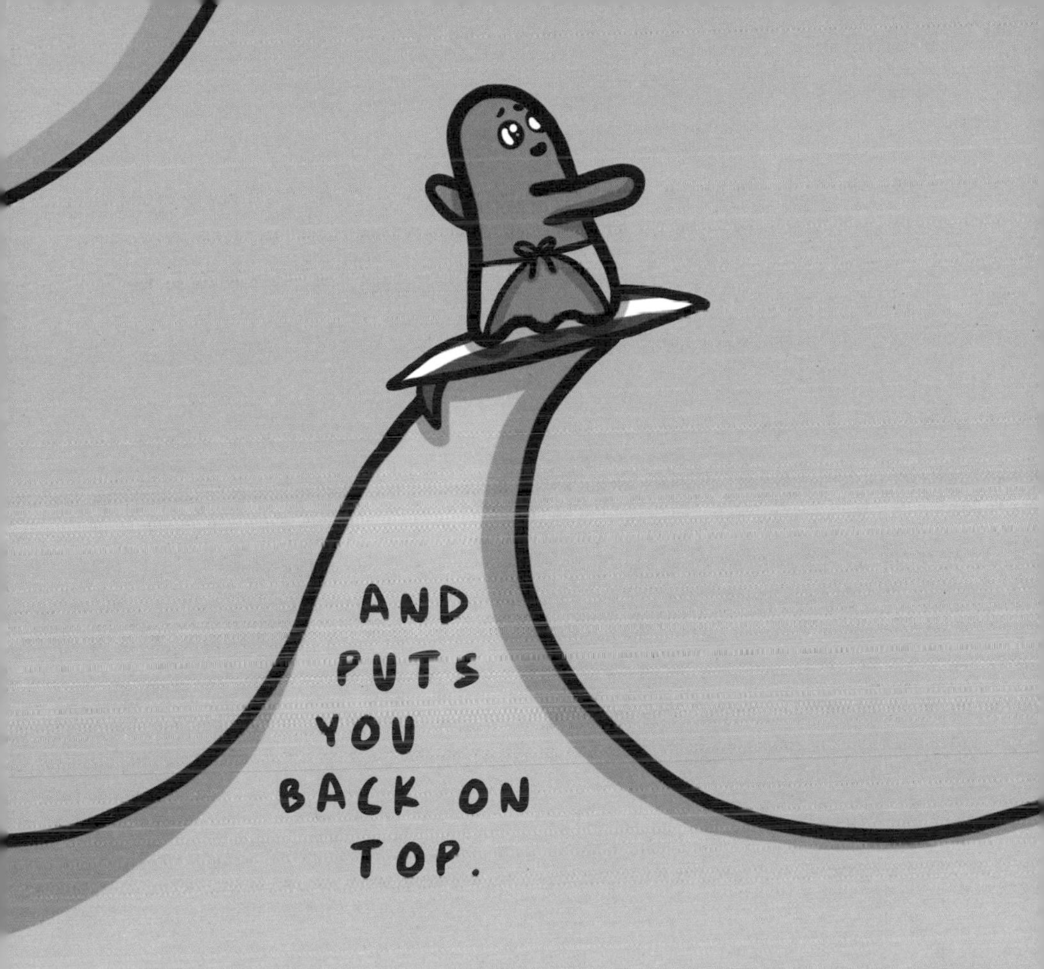

AND PUTS YOU BACK ON TOP.

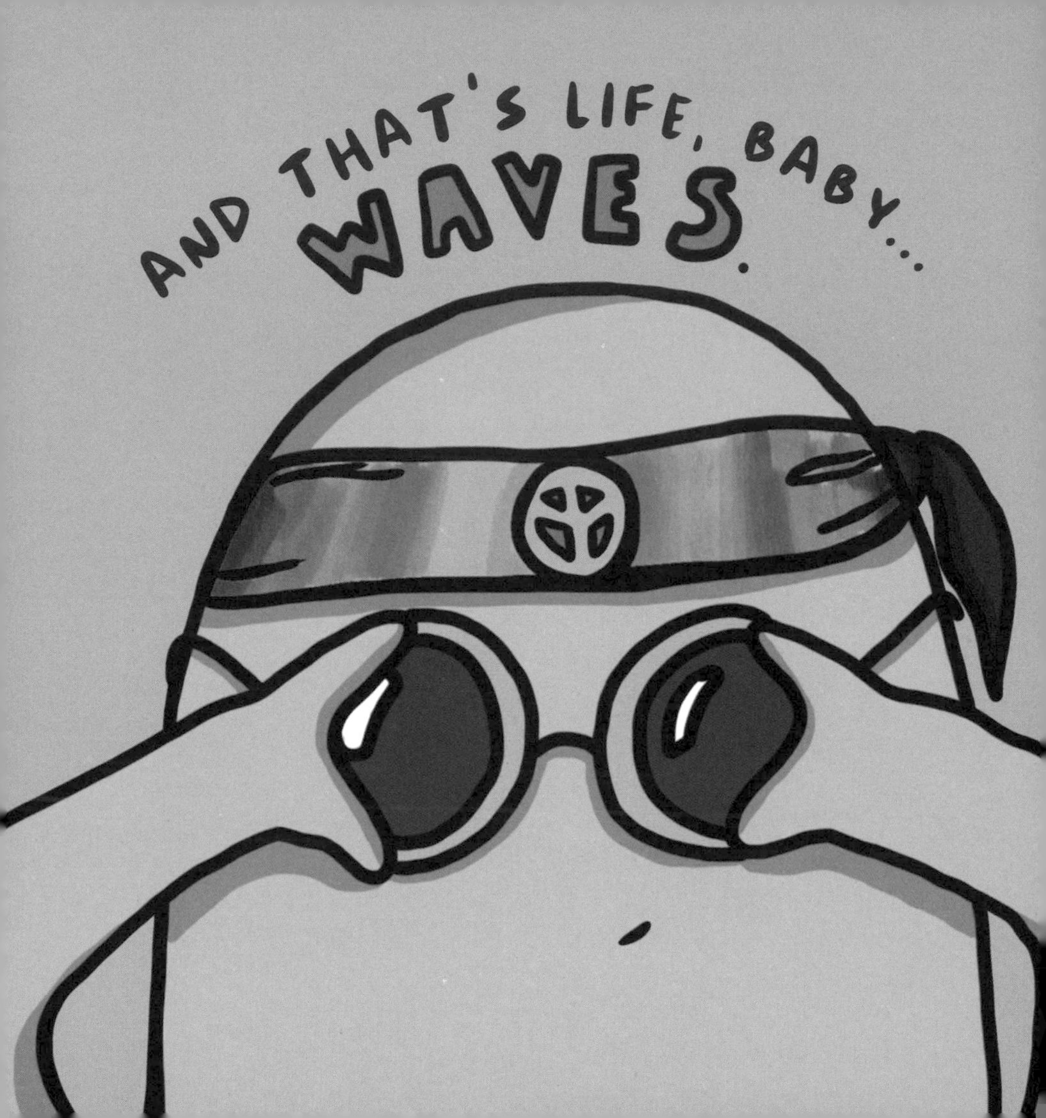
AND THAT'S LIFE, BABY...
WAVES.

THE TOILET BOWL OF REGRET

27

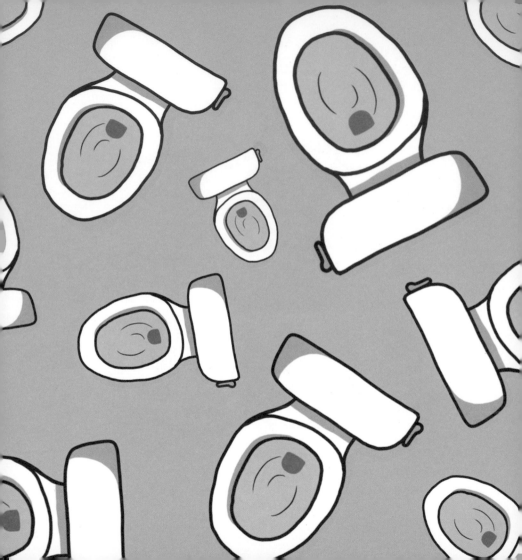

IF YOU'RE SWIRLING

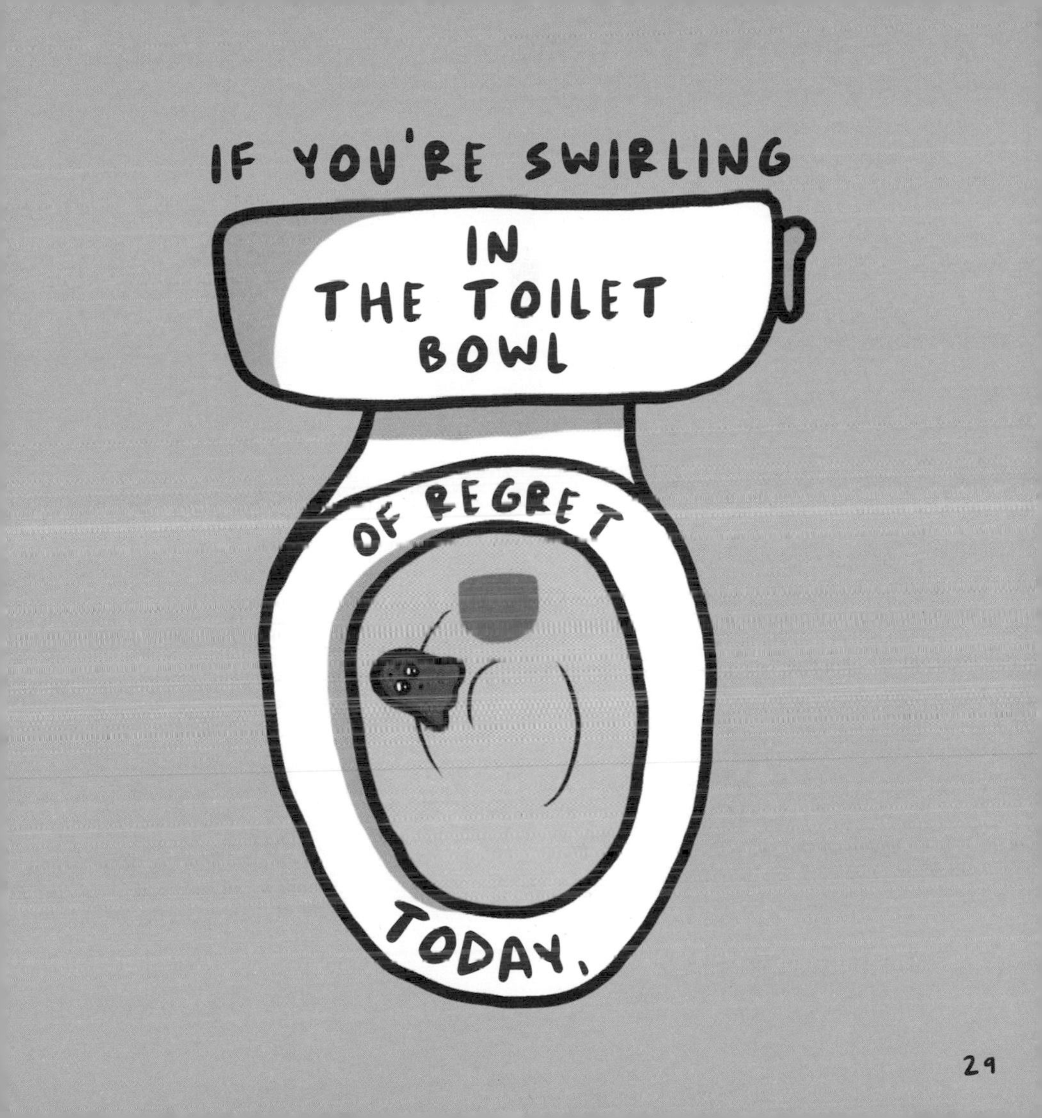
IN
THE TOILET
BOWL
OF REGRET
TODAY,

THIS IS YOUR REMINDER TO:

TRY TO SHIFT YOUR OUTLOOK

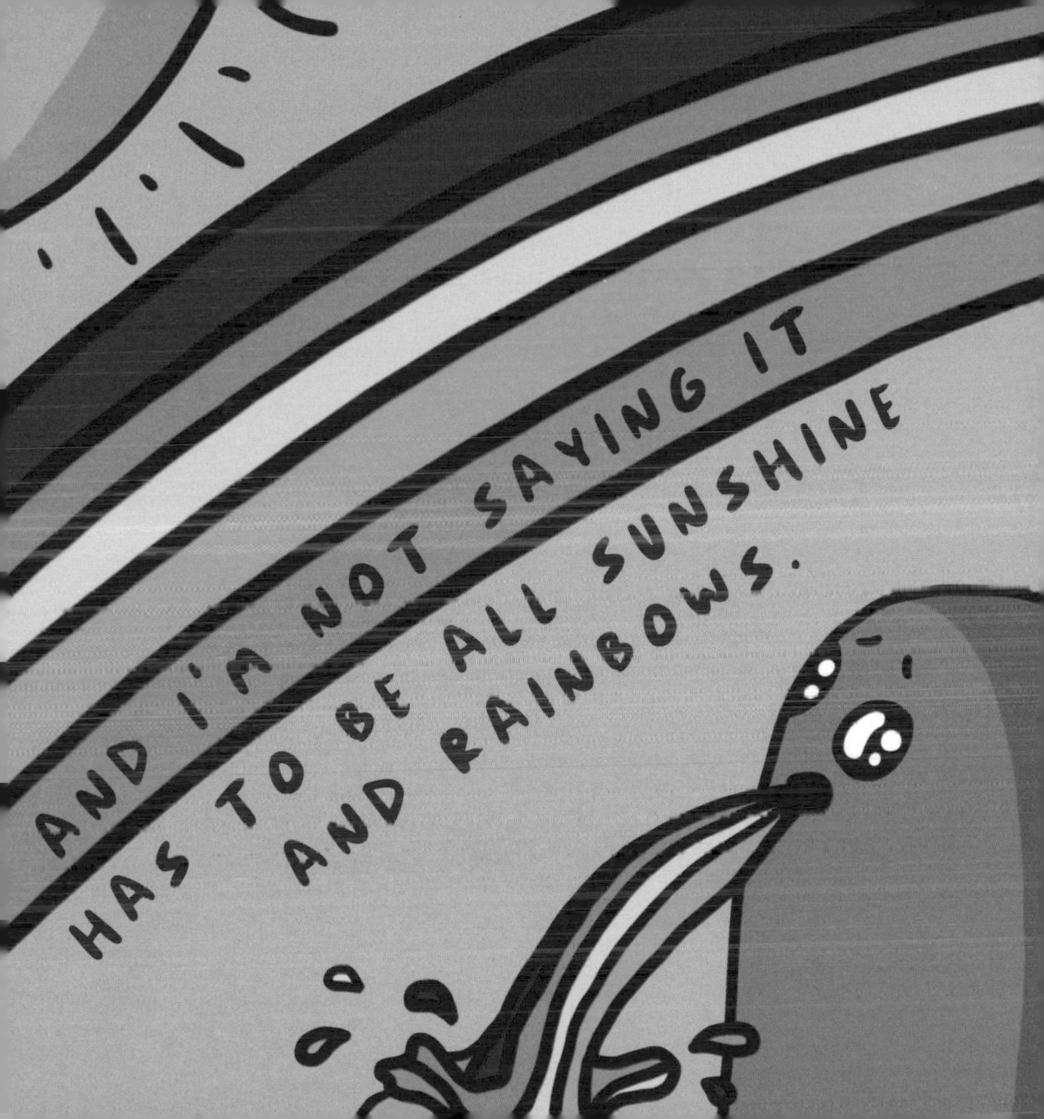
AND I'M NOT SAYING IT
HAS TO BE ALL SUNSHINE
AND RAINBOWS.

♡ ♡ ♡

JUST SOMETHING THAT
DOESN'T INTENTIONALLY
KEEP YOU TRAPPED IN
A HARMFUL THOUGHT
PATTERN ALL DAY.

OKAY, FOR EXAMPLE...

LET'S SAY
YOU SAY
SOMETHING
STUPID

(AS WE ALL DO, LOL)

YOU COULD

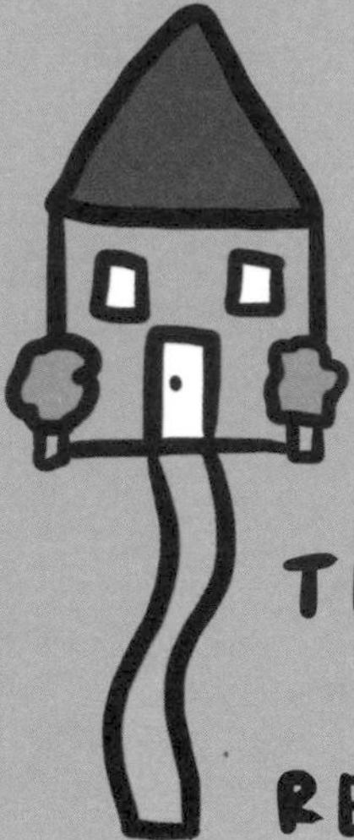

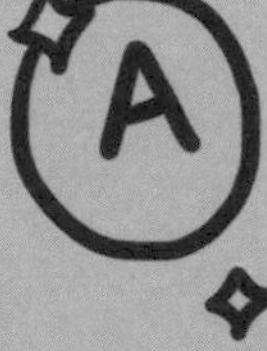
A

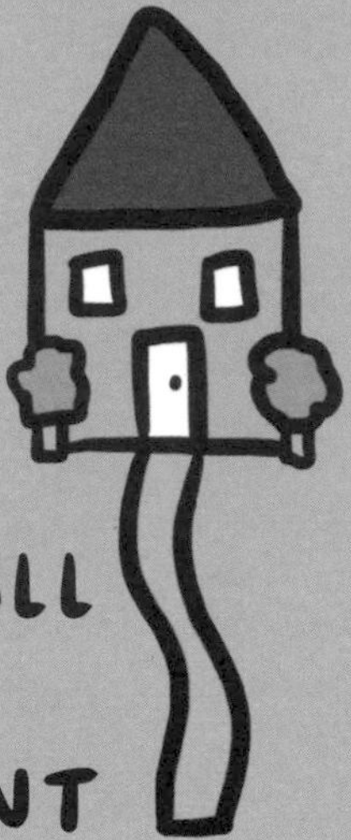

GO HOME,
THINK ABOUT IT ALL NIGHT,
REPLAY THE MOMENT IN YOUR HEAD OVER AND OVER AND OVER AND OVER.

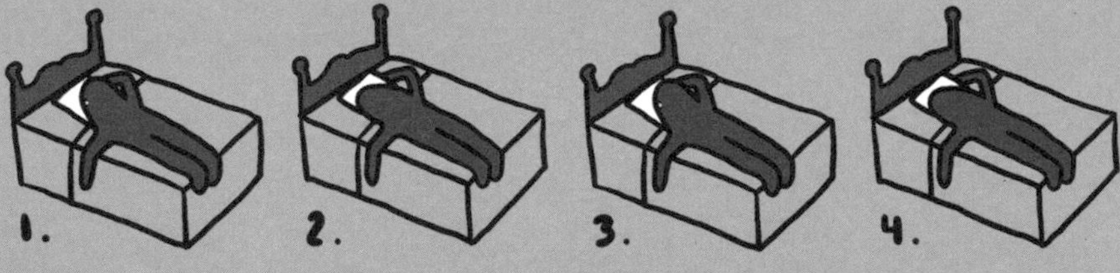
1.
2.
3.
4.

OR!

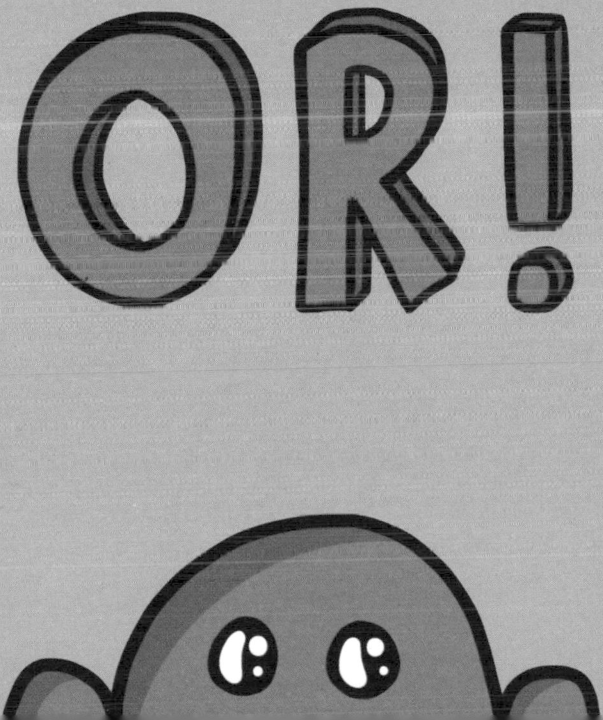

YOU COULD

B

BE LIKE,

YEAH, I SAID SOMETHING

STUPID

BUT, YOU KNOW, WHO REMEMBERS?

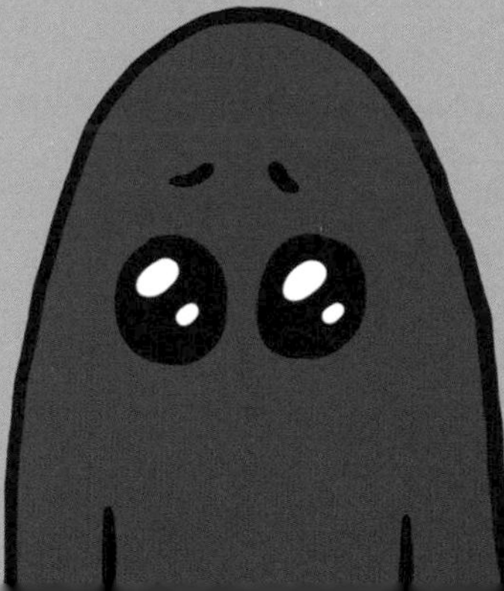

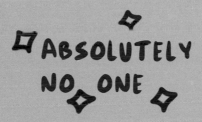

ABSOLUTELY
NO ONE

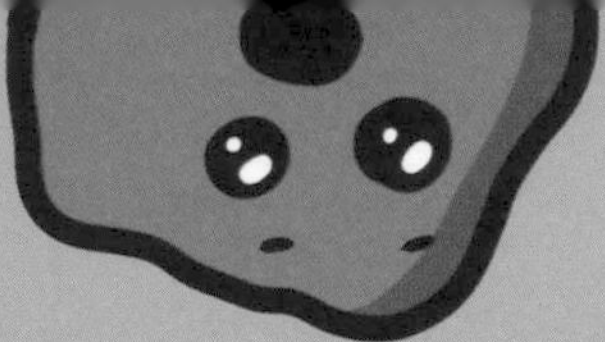

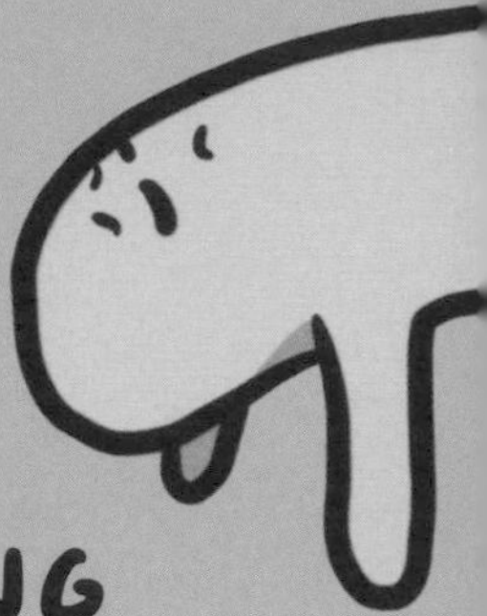

BECAUSE EVERY SINGLE PERSON I'M WORRYING ABOUT IS ALSO SITTING AT HOME WORRYING ABOUT THAT STUPID THING THEY SAID TO SOMEONE ELSE...

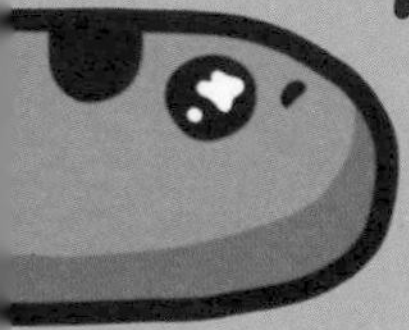

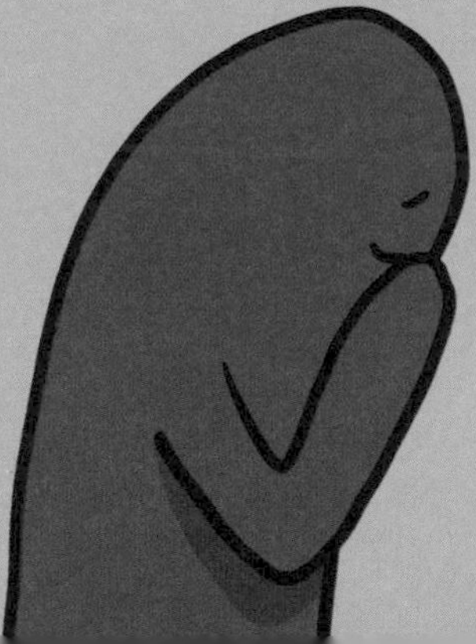

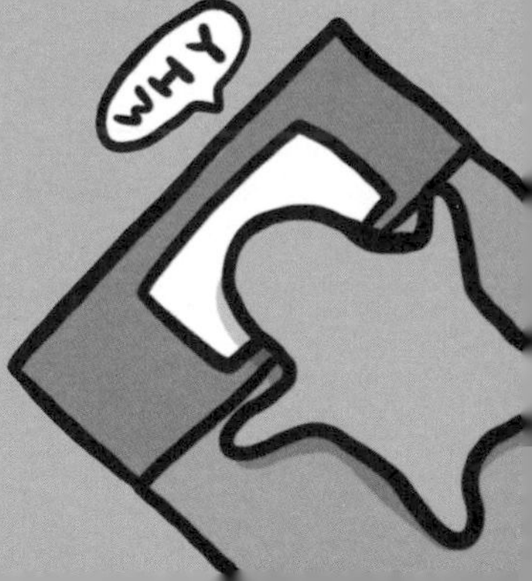
WHY

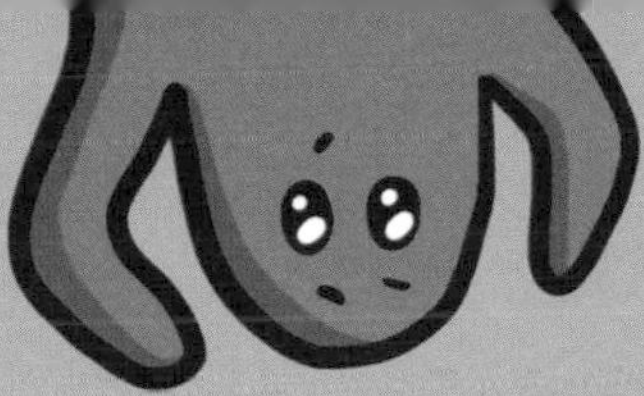

THE EGOTISTICAL HUMAN CONDITION IS SOMETIMES A BEAUTIFUL THING WHEN USED FOR THE RIGHT PURPOSE!

ANYWAY,

♥

❖NOTHING
IS AS BIG A
DEAL AS WE
MAKE IT OUT
TO BE IN OUR
MINDS.❖

THAT I KNOW FOR SURE.

♥

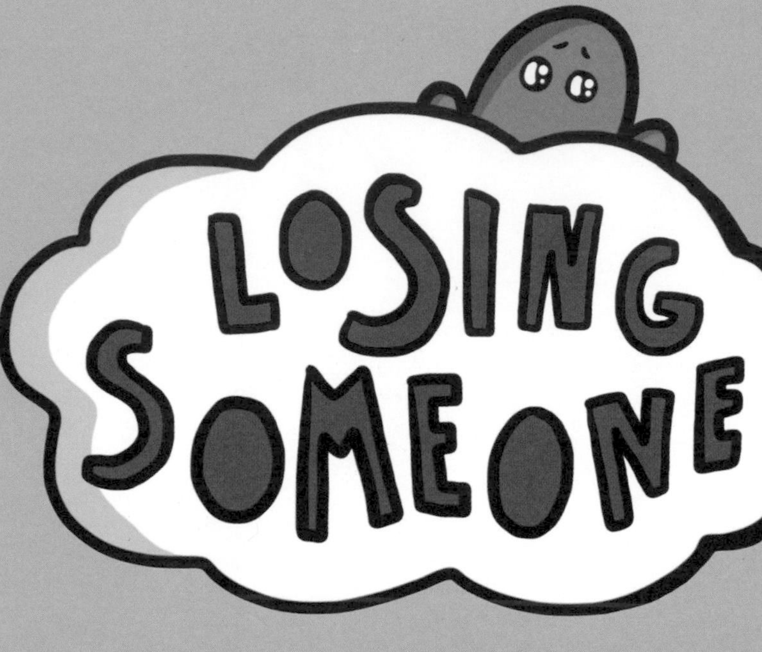
LOSING
SOMEONE

PEOPLE COME INTO OUR LIVES,

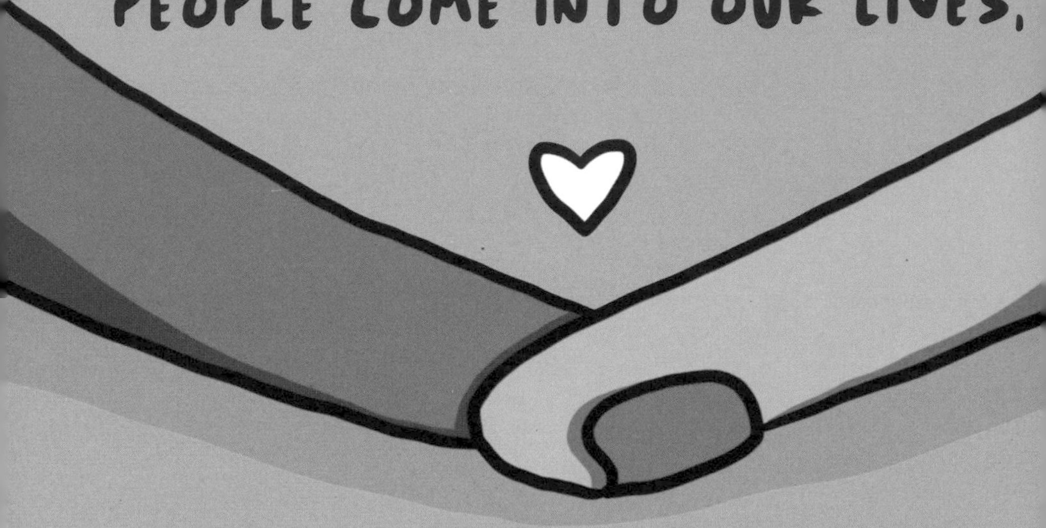

AND YOU NEVER KNOW FOR HOW LONG.

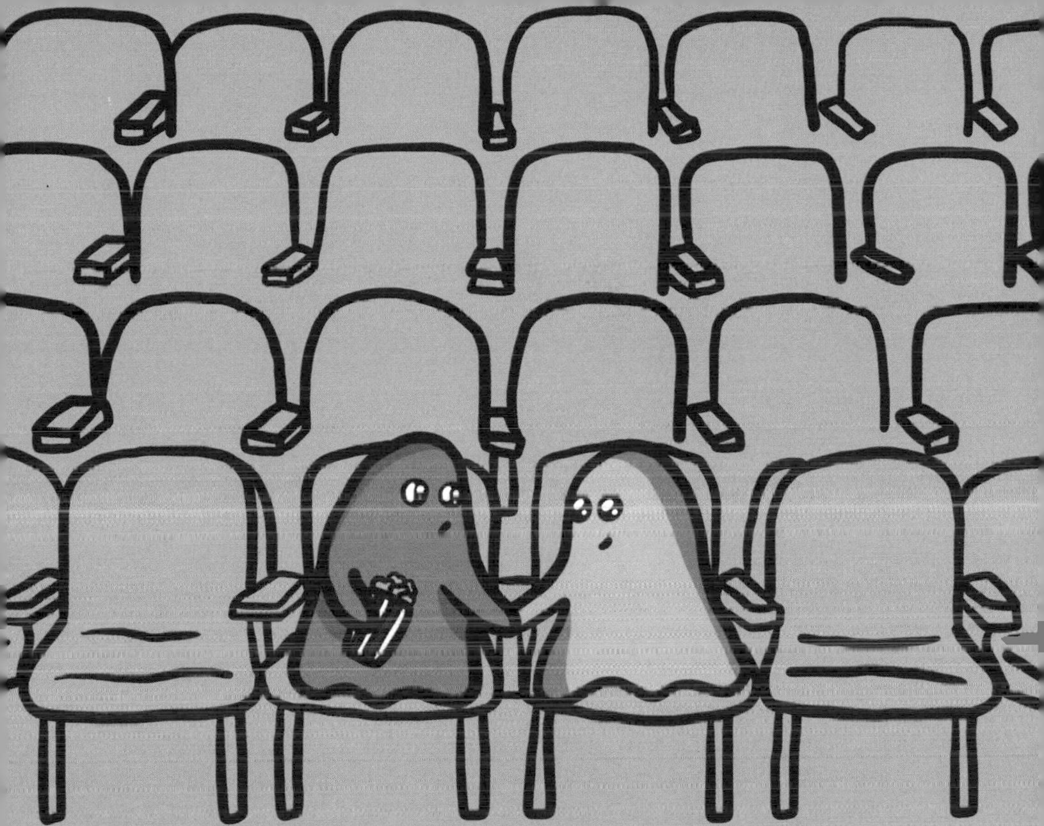

SOMETIMES THEY LEAVE
AT THE END OF
THE MOVIE,

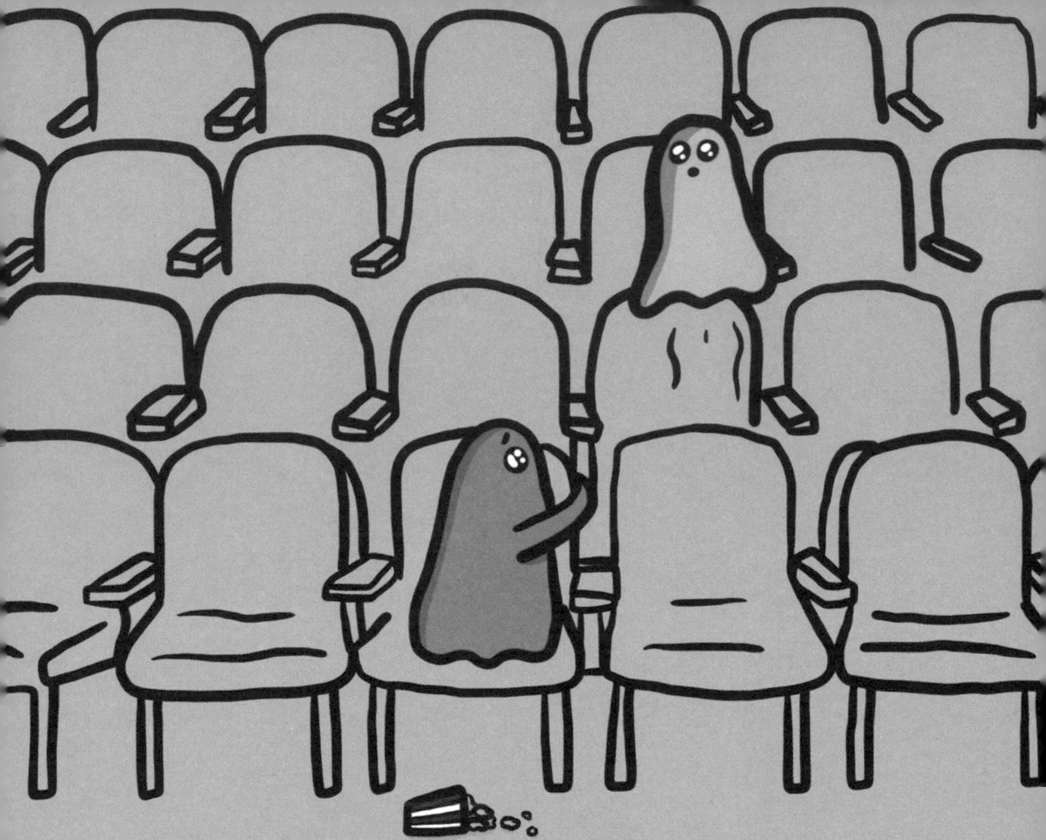

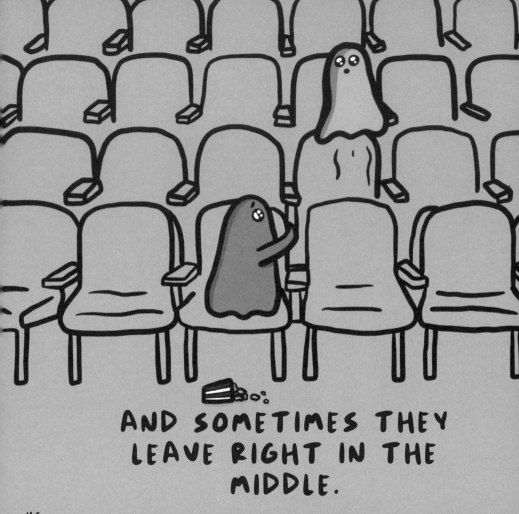

AND SOMETIMES THEY LEAVE RIGHT IN THE MIDDLE.

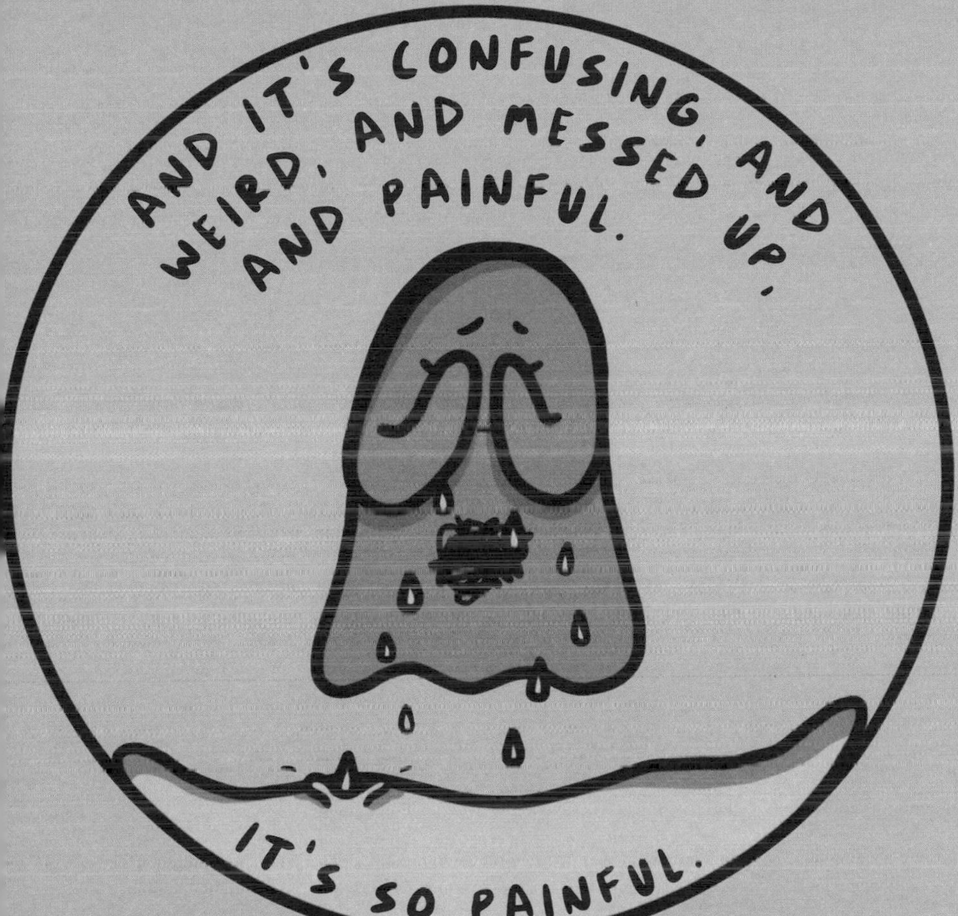
AND IT'S CONFUSING, AND
WEIRD, AND MESSED UP,
AND PAINFUL.
IT'S SO PAINFUL.

BUT I WANT YOU TO LOOK
AT PAIN AS THIS THING,
THIS TANGIBLE THING.

LET'S SAY PAIN IS A...

BOX.

WHEN YOU TAKE THE BOX OUT OF YOUR CHEST AND YOU OPEN IT UP,

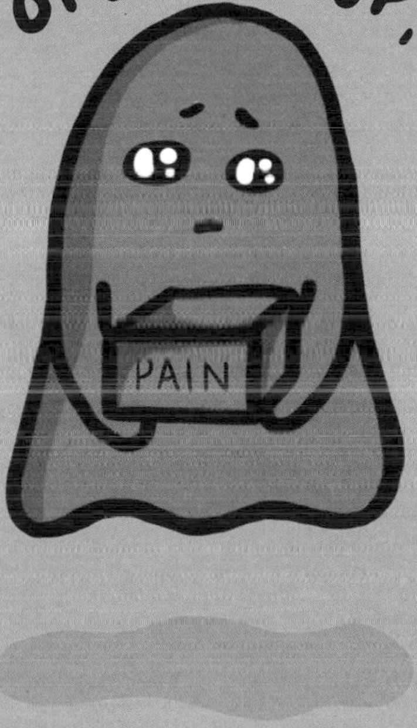
PAIN

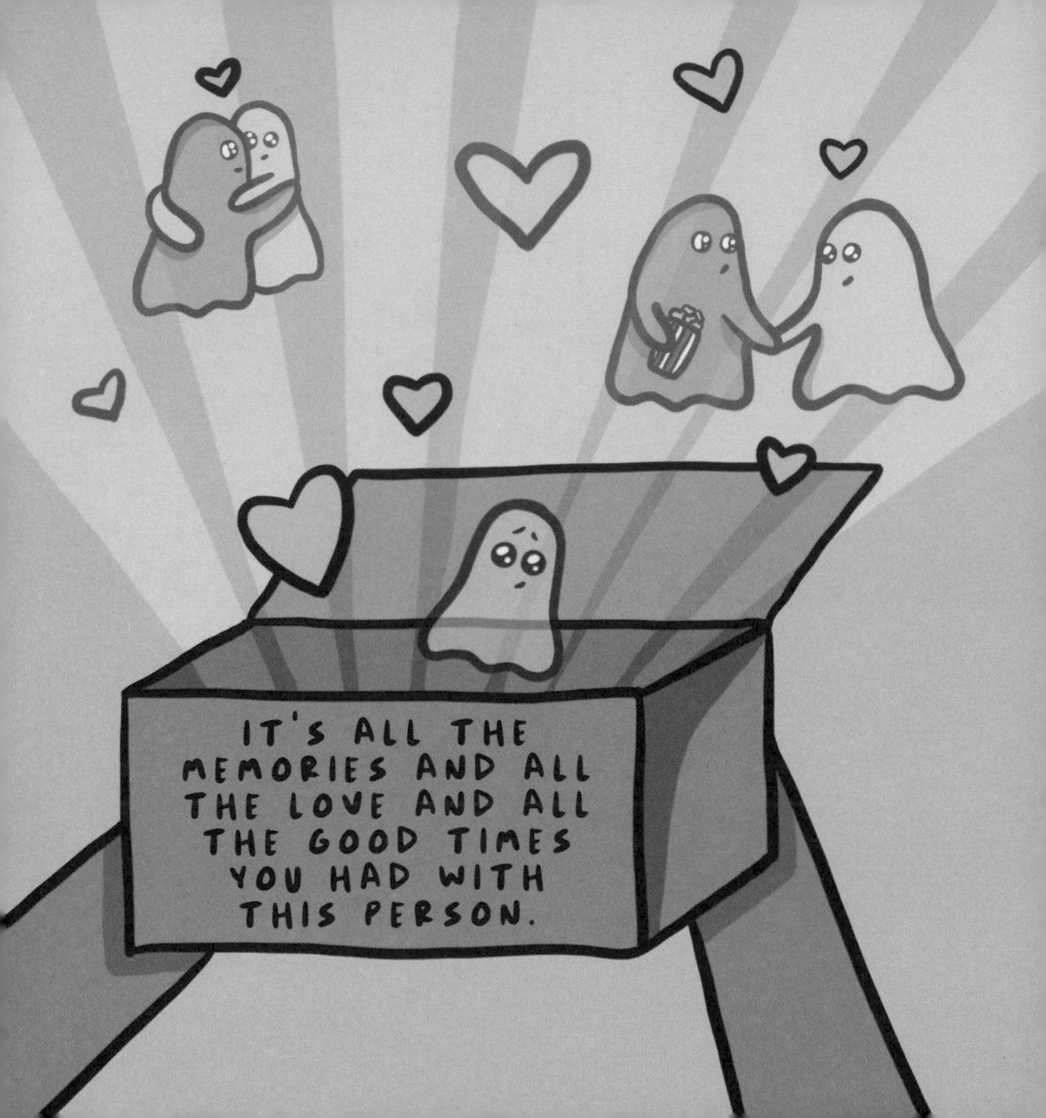
IT'S ALL THE MEMORIES AND ALL THE LOVE AND ALL THE GOOD TIMES YOU HAD WITH THIS PERSON.

THE BOX MAY
BE DARK
AND GREY ON
THE OUTSIDE,

BUT THE INSIDE
IS BEAUTIFUL,
BECAUSE THE BOX
IS THE REMINDER
THAT

THEY
WERE
REAL.

I KNOW THIS IS SO HARD, BUT I ALSO KNOW THAT YOU GOT THIS.

I BELIEVE IN YOU AND I LOVE YOU!

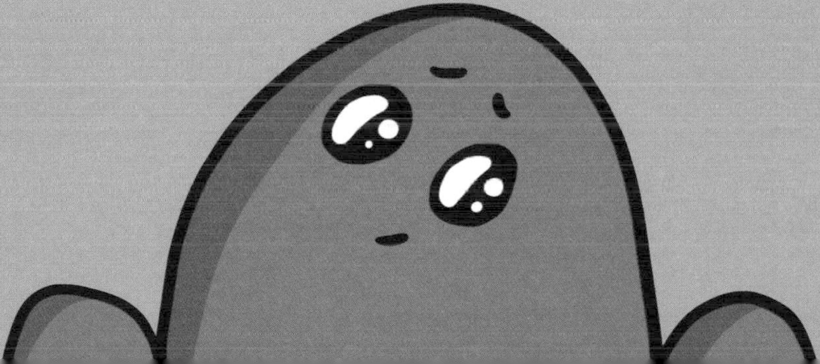

II

The Failing

♥

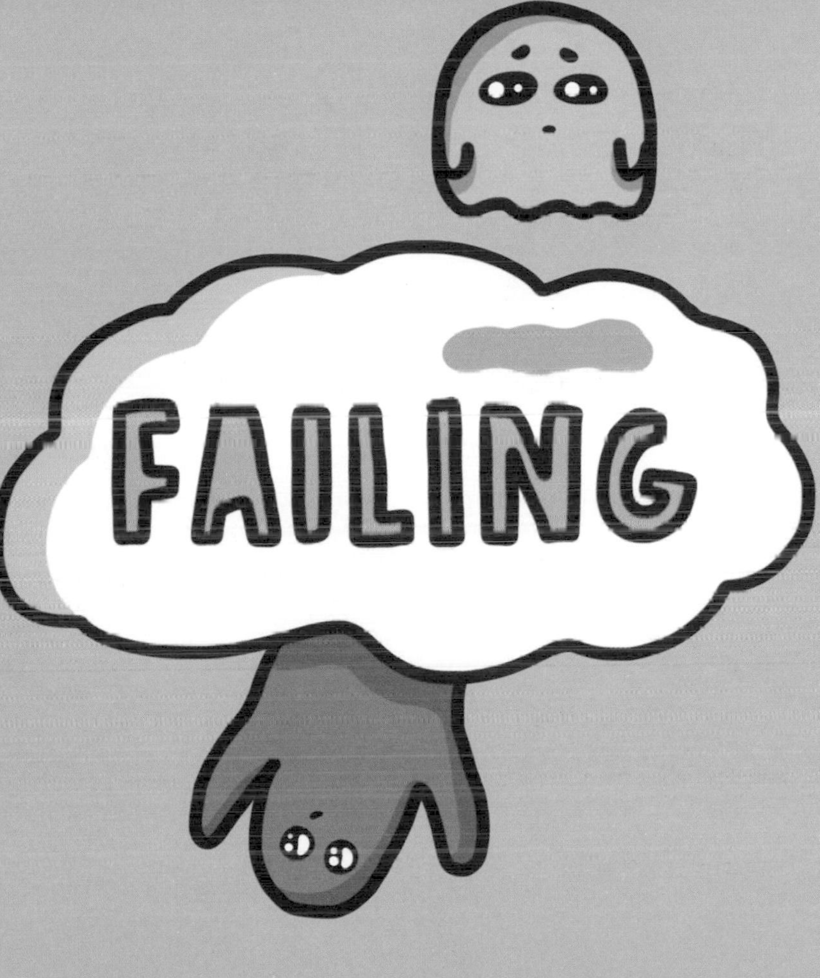
FAILING

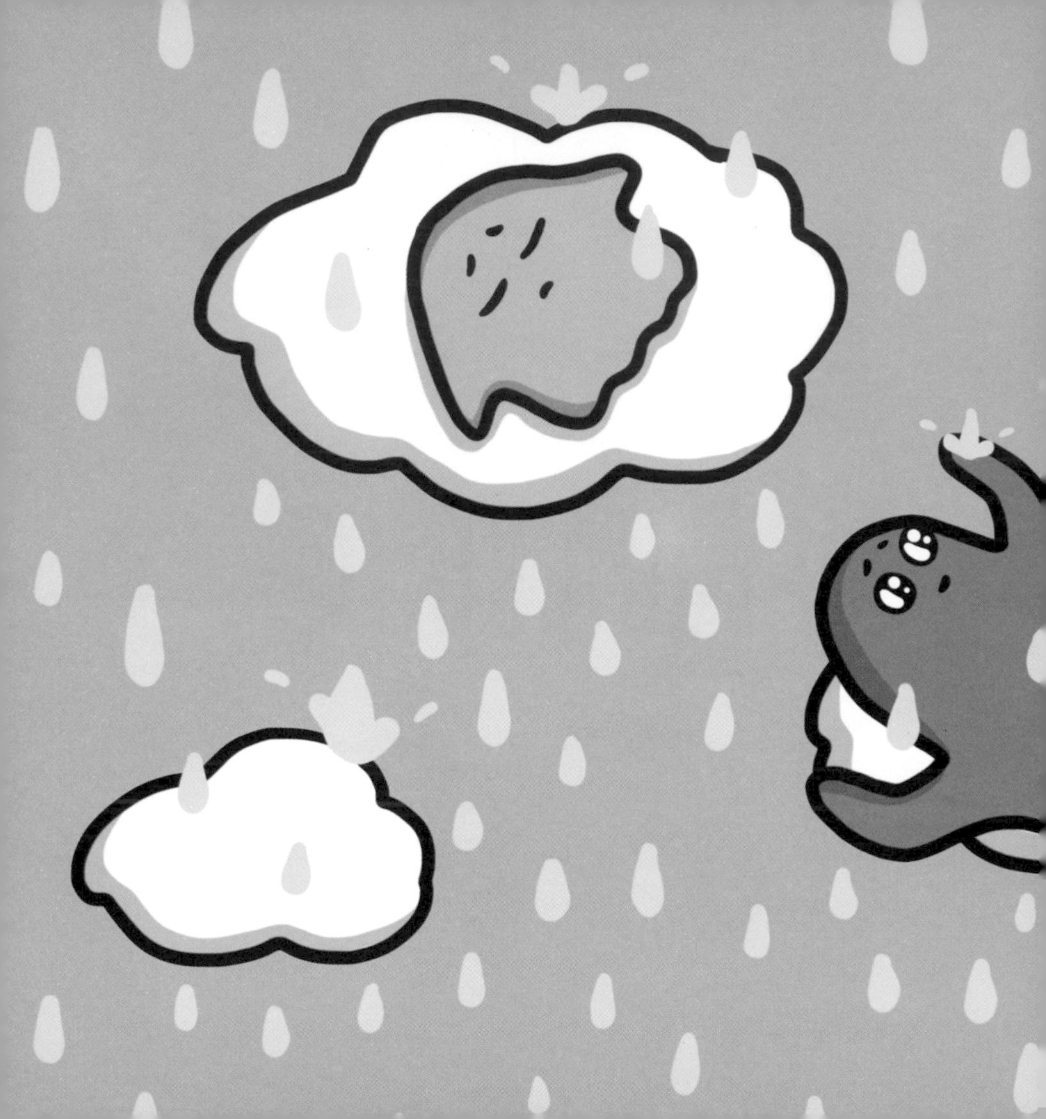

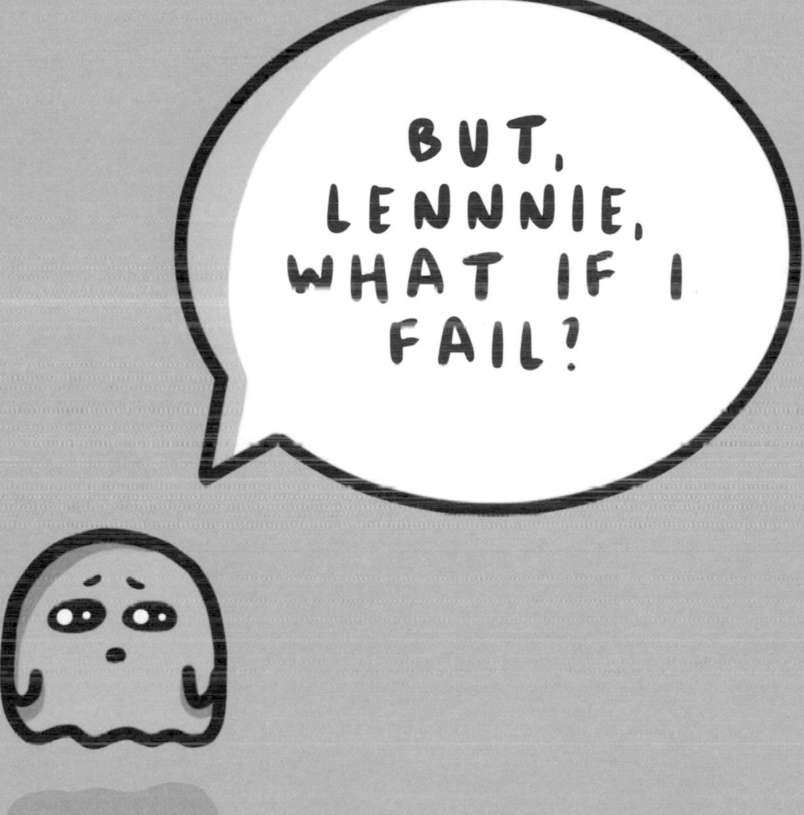
BUT, LENNNIE, WHAT IF I FAIL?

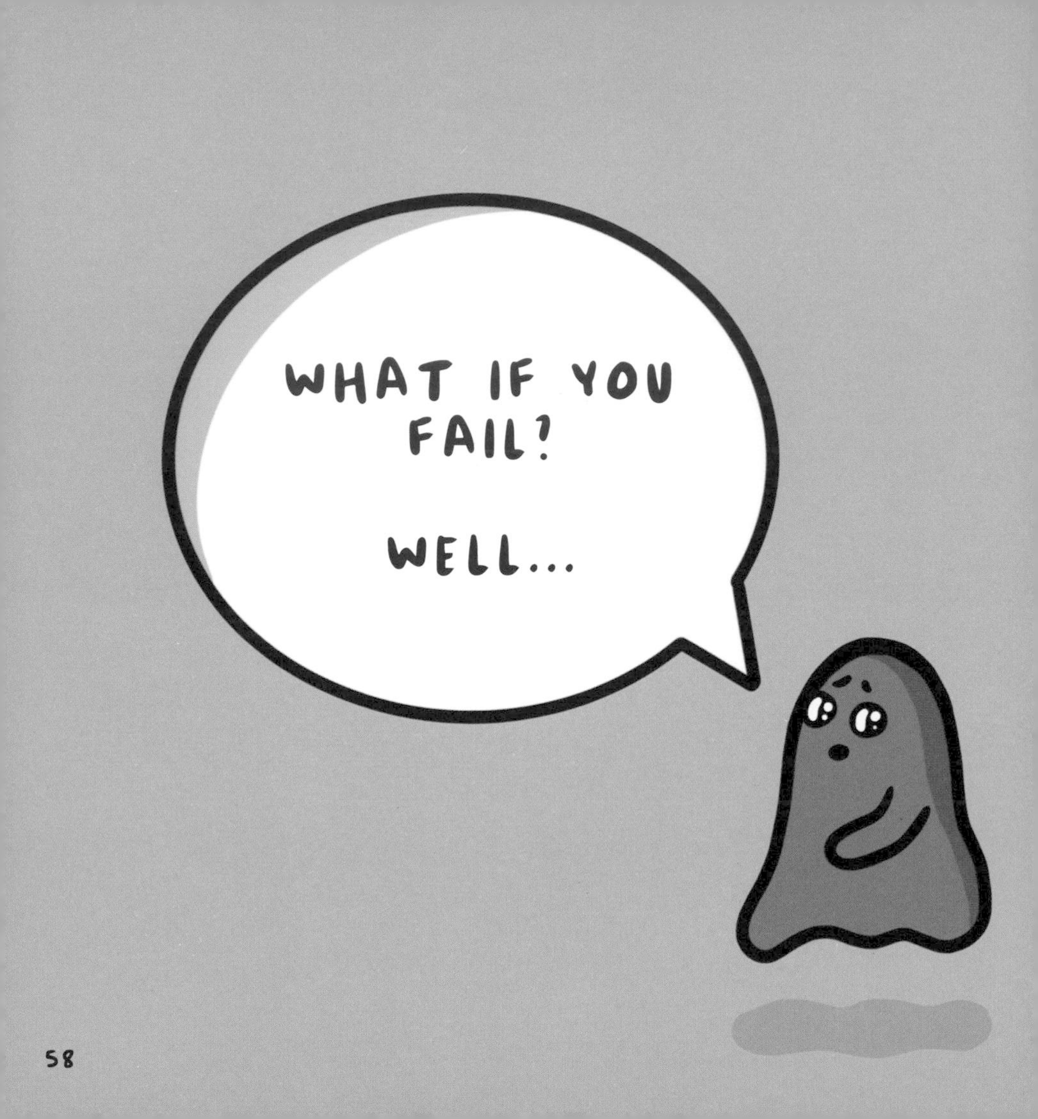
WHAT IF YOU FAIL?
WELL...

IF YOU FAIL?
YOU ALREADY WON,
BECAUSE
YOU TRIED IN THE FIRST PLACE.

DO YOU KNOW
HOW MANY PEOPLE
WANTED TO TRY
BUT DIDN'T
BECAUSE THEY WERE
TOO SCARED?

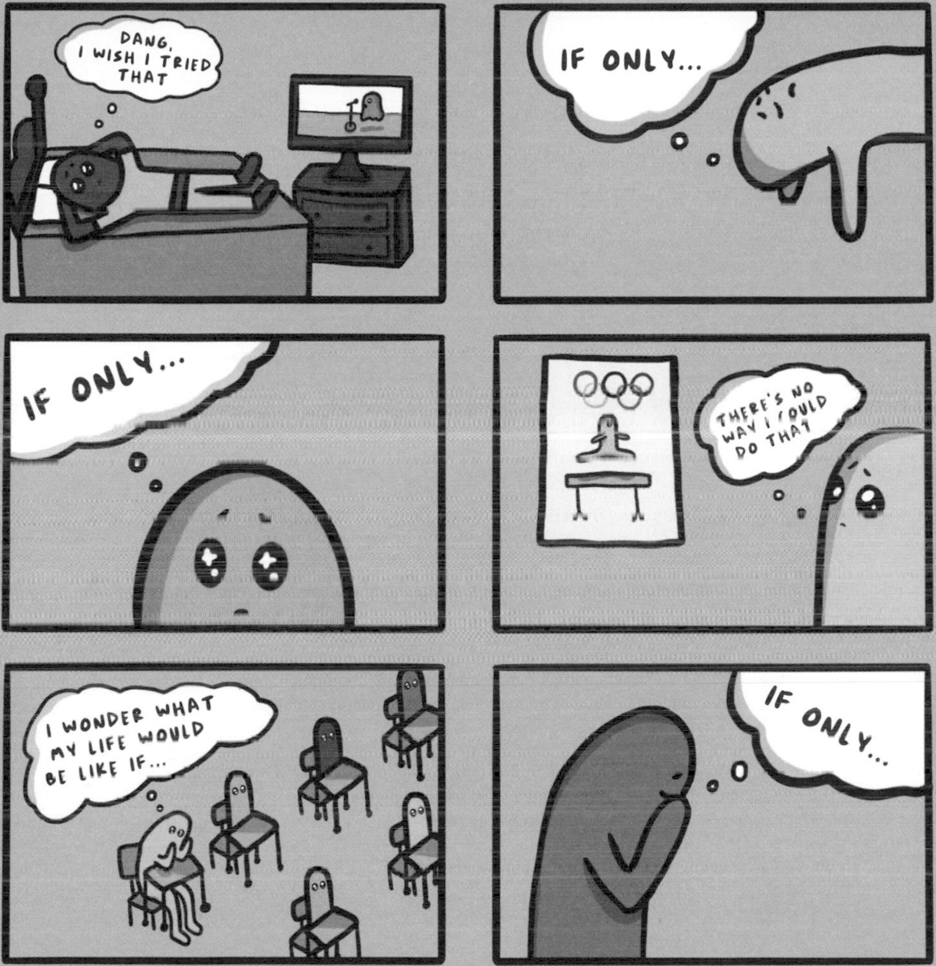
DANG, I WISH I TRIED THAT
IF ONLY...
IF ONLY...
THERE'S NO WAY I COULD DO THAT
I WONDER WHAT MY LIFE WOULD BE LIKE IF...
IF ONLY...

SO MANY.

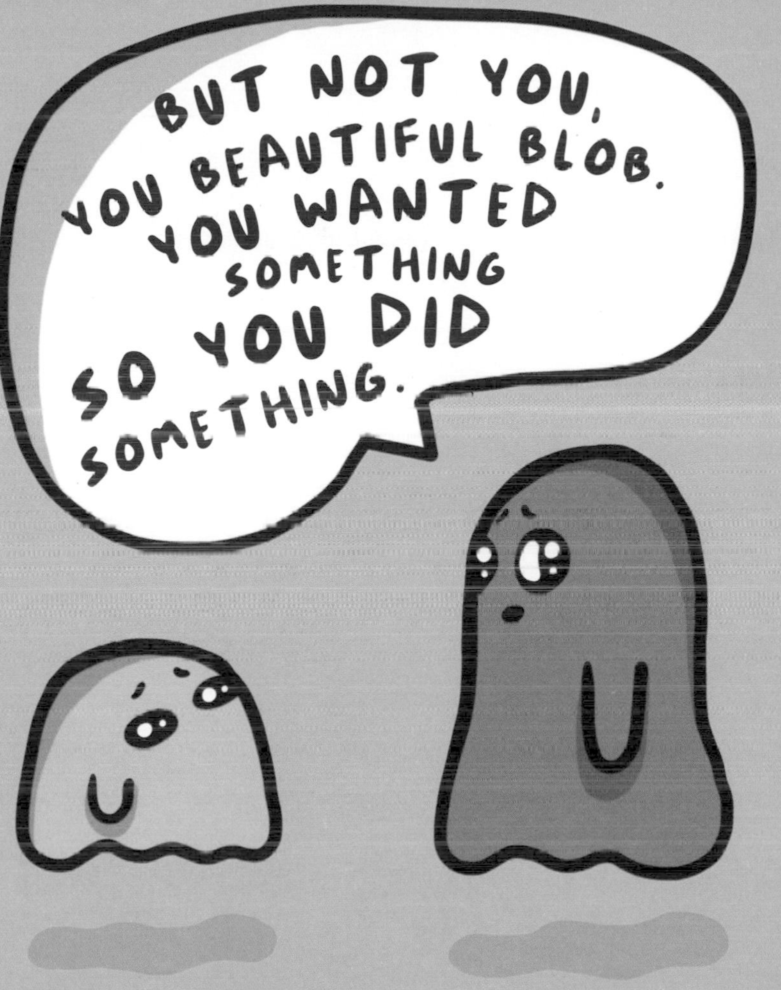
BUT NOT YOU,
YOU BEAUTIFUL BLOB.
YOU WANTED
SOMETHING
SO YOU DID
SOMETHING.

IF THAT DOESN'T MAKE SOMEONE WORTHY,

I HONESTLY DON'T KNOW WHAT DOES.

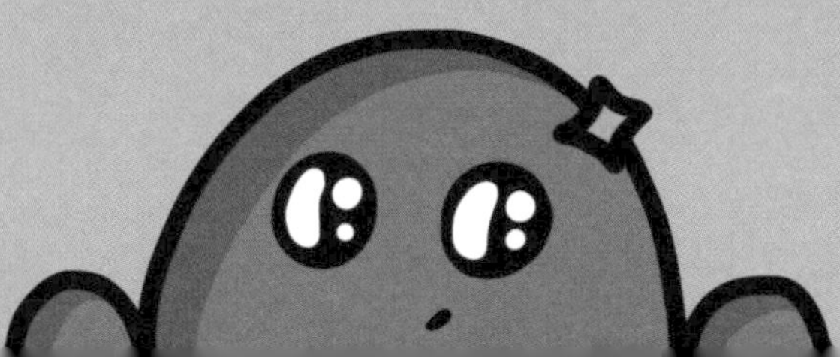

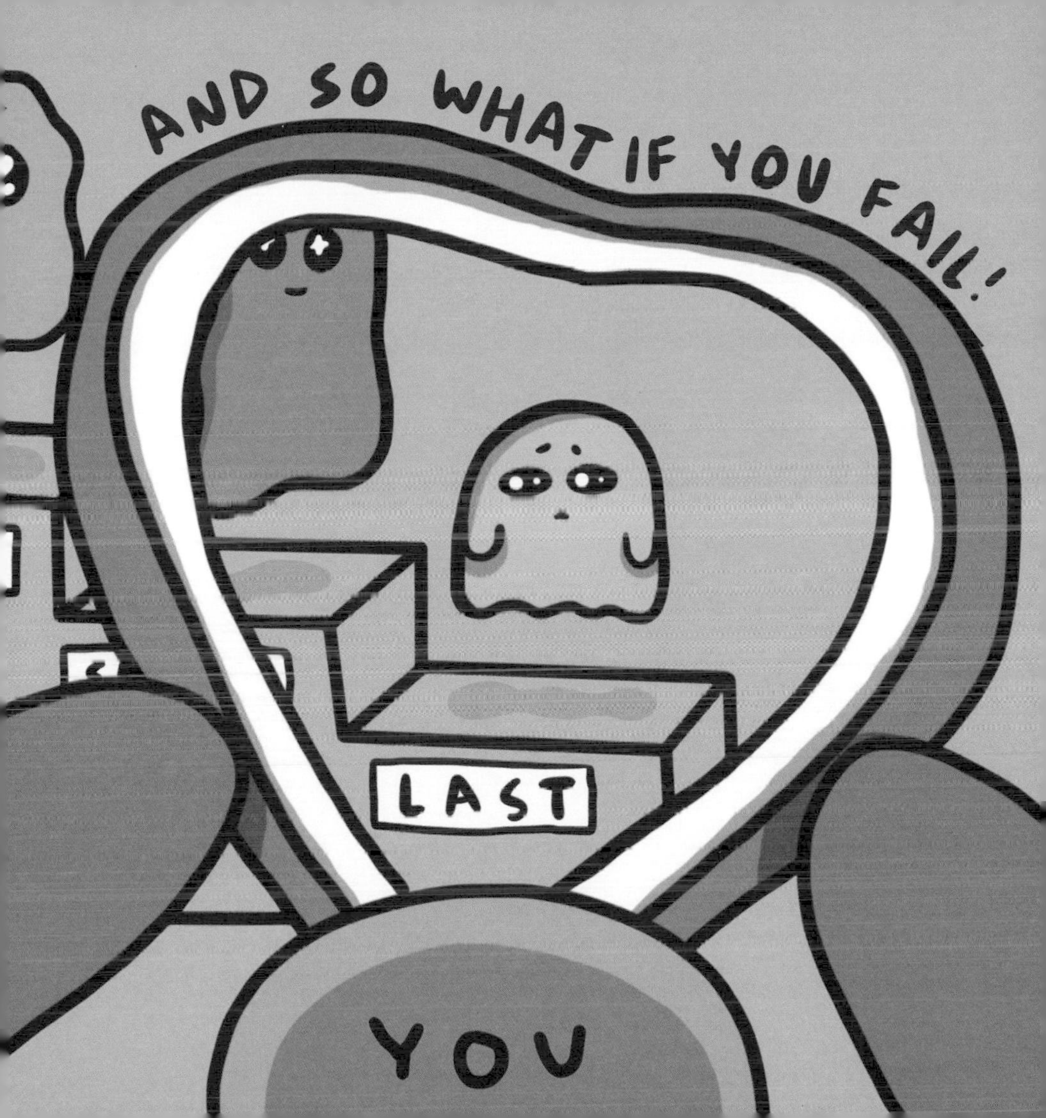
AND SO WHAT IF YOU FAIL!
LAST
YOU

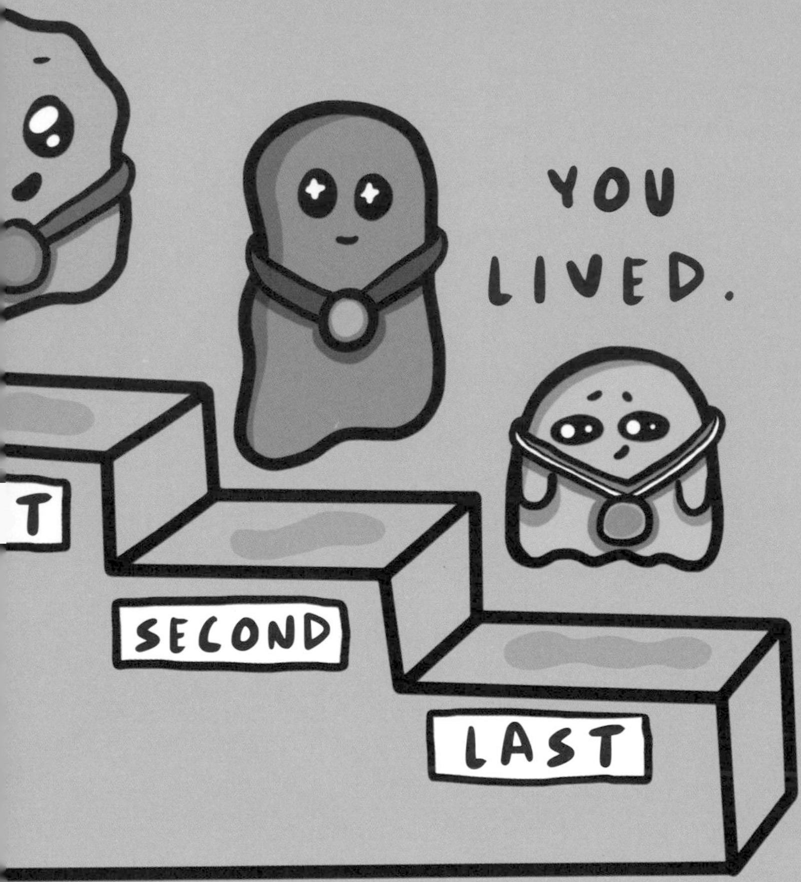
YOU LIVED.
T
SECOND
LAST

I CAN'T WAIT TO SEE

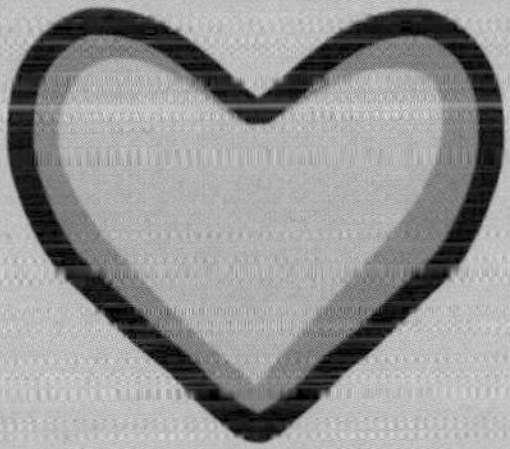

WHAT YOU DO!

WHEN THINGS DON'T GO YOUR WAY

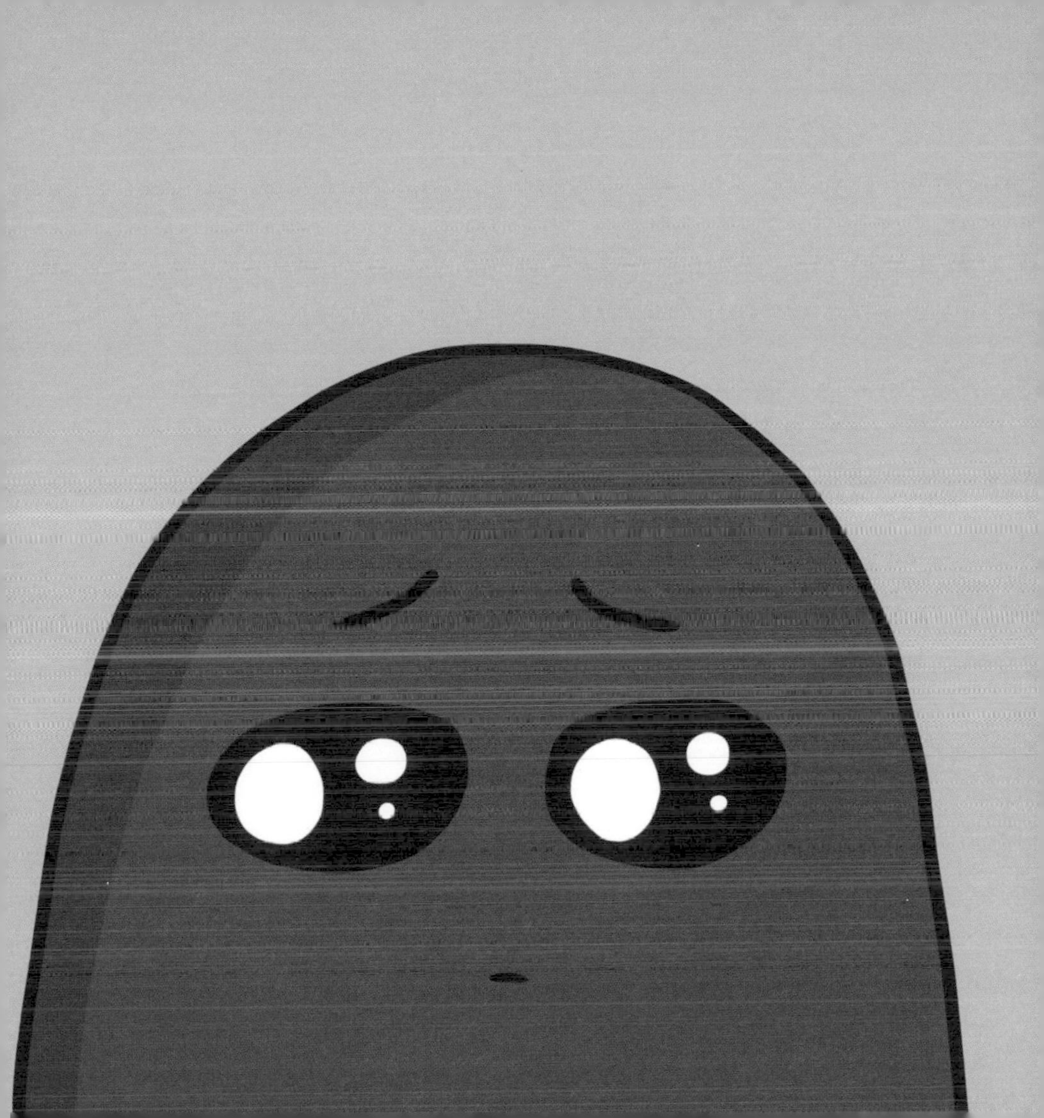

WHEN THINGS
DON'T PAN OUT THE
WAY YOU WANT
THEM TO,

YOU'RE GONNA BE CONFUSED,
AND SAD,

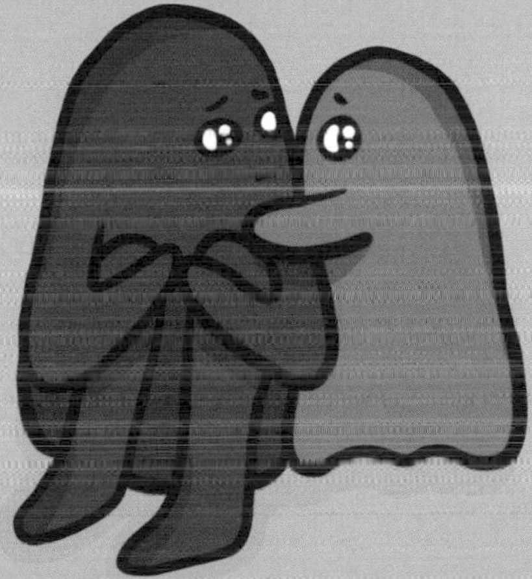

AND PISSED AT THE WORLD.

AND

YES!

ABSOLUTELY
BE
THAT.

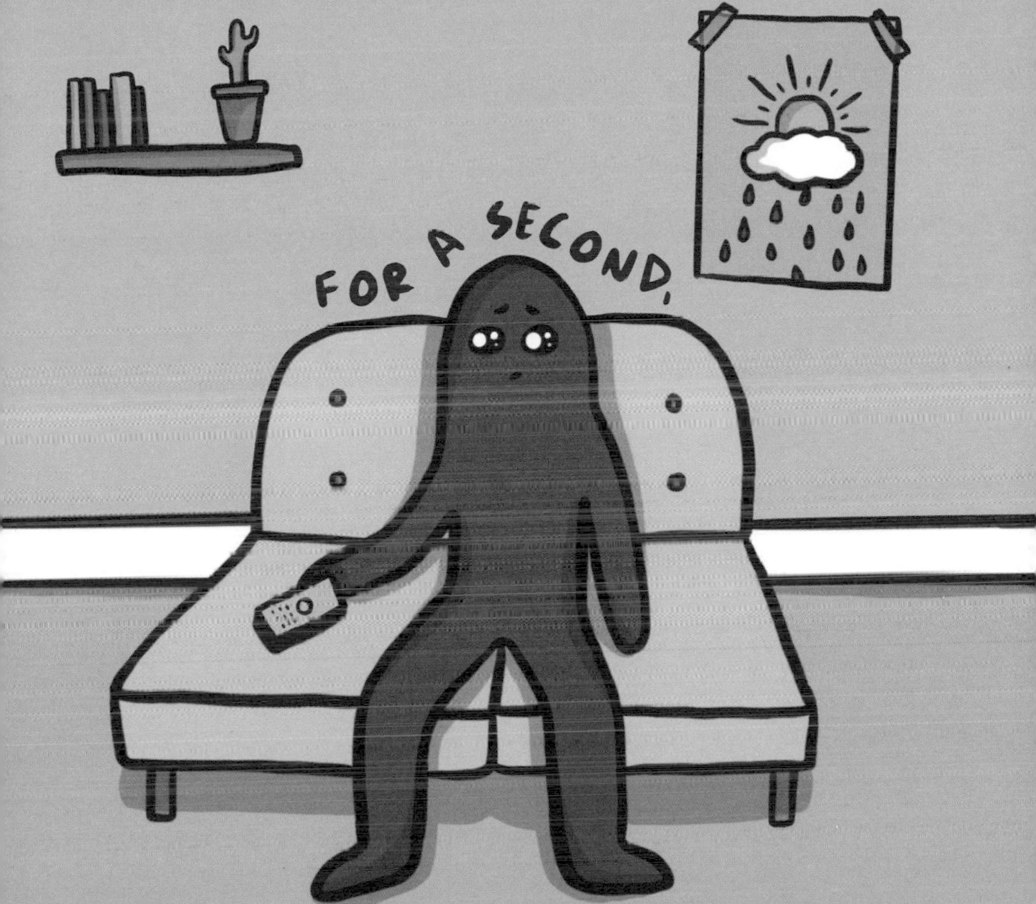
FOR A SECOND,

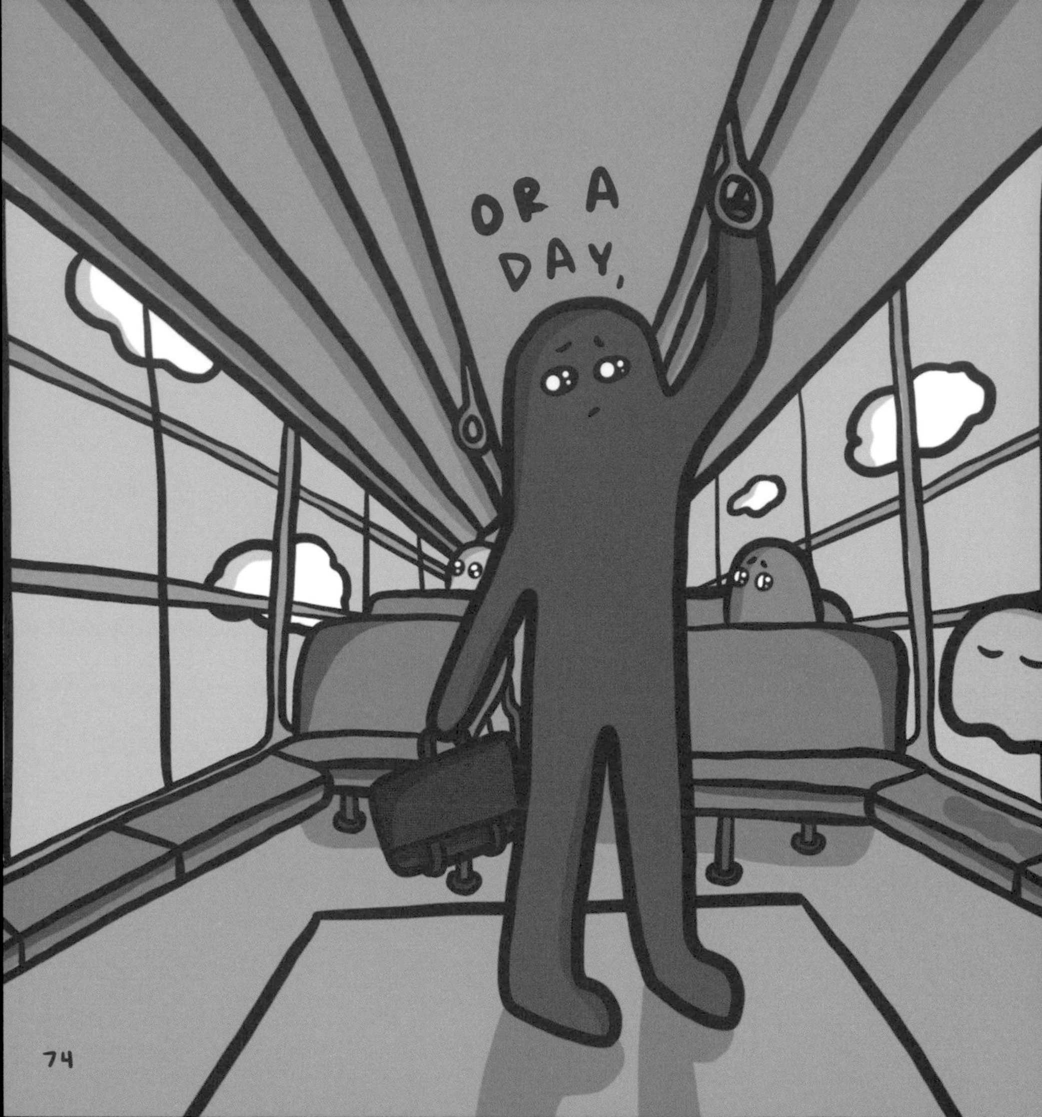
OR A DAY,

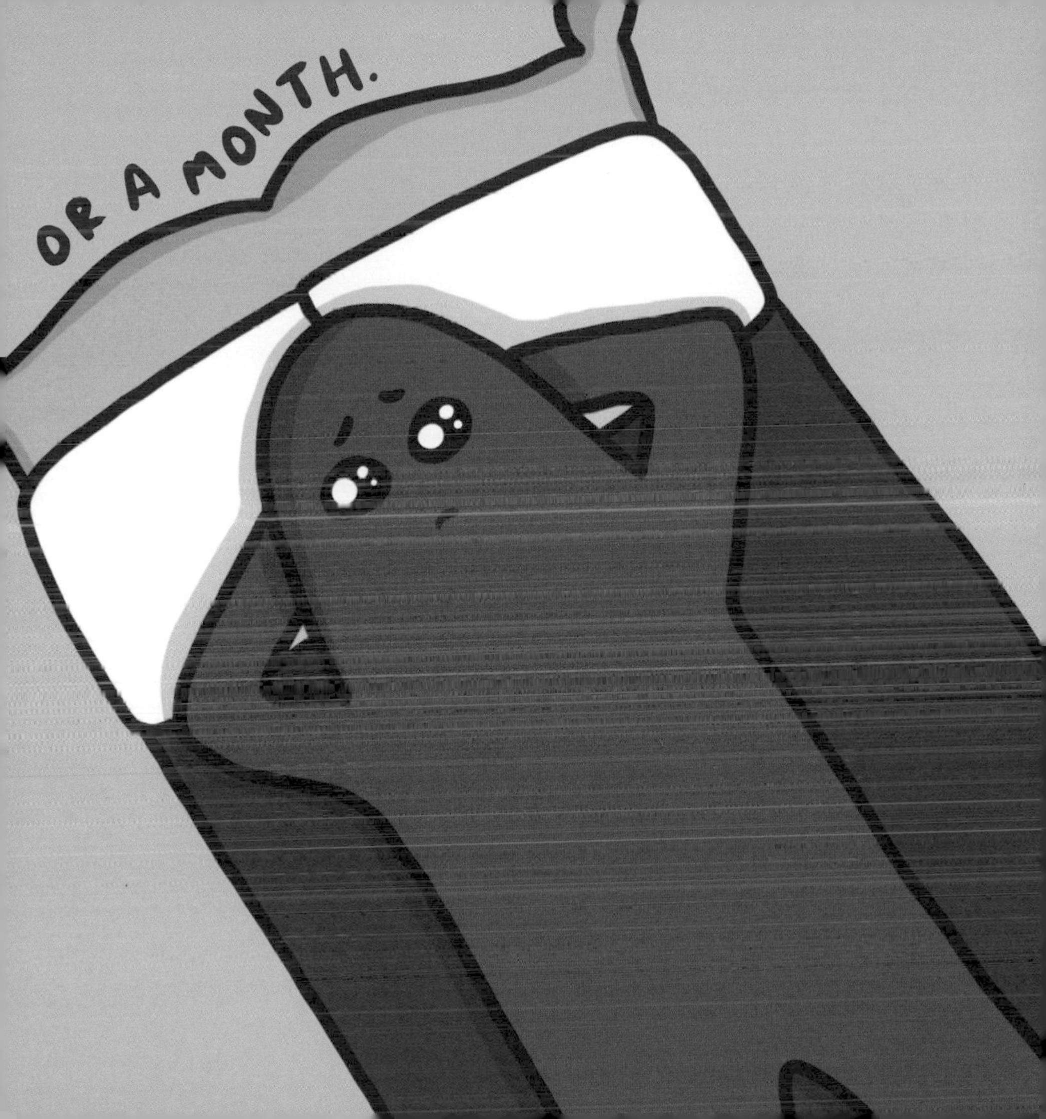
OR A MONTH.

BUT
DO NOT
LET IT
CONSUME
YOU.

DO NOT LET IT BECOME A PART OF WHO YOU ARE.

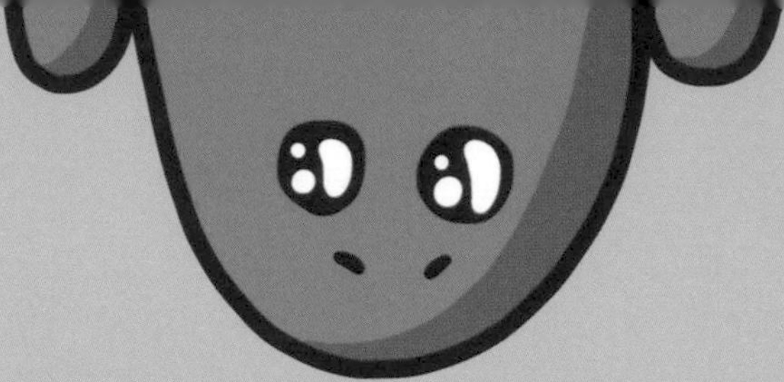

IT DOESN'T DESERVE THAT PERMANENT SPOT IN YOUR LIFE.

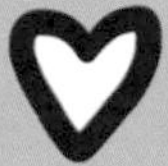

AND IT DEFINITELY DOESN'T DESERVE TO HOLD THAT SPOT IN YOUR MIND.

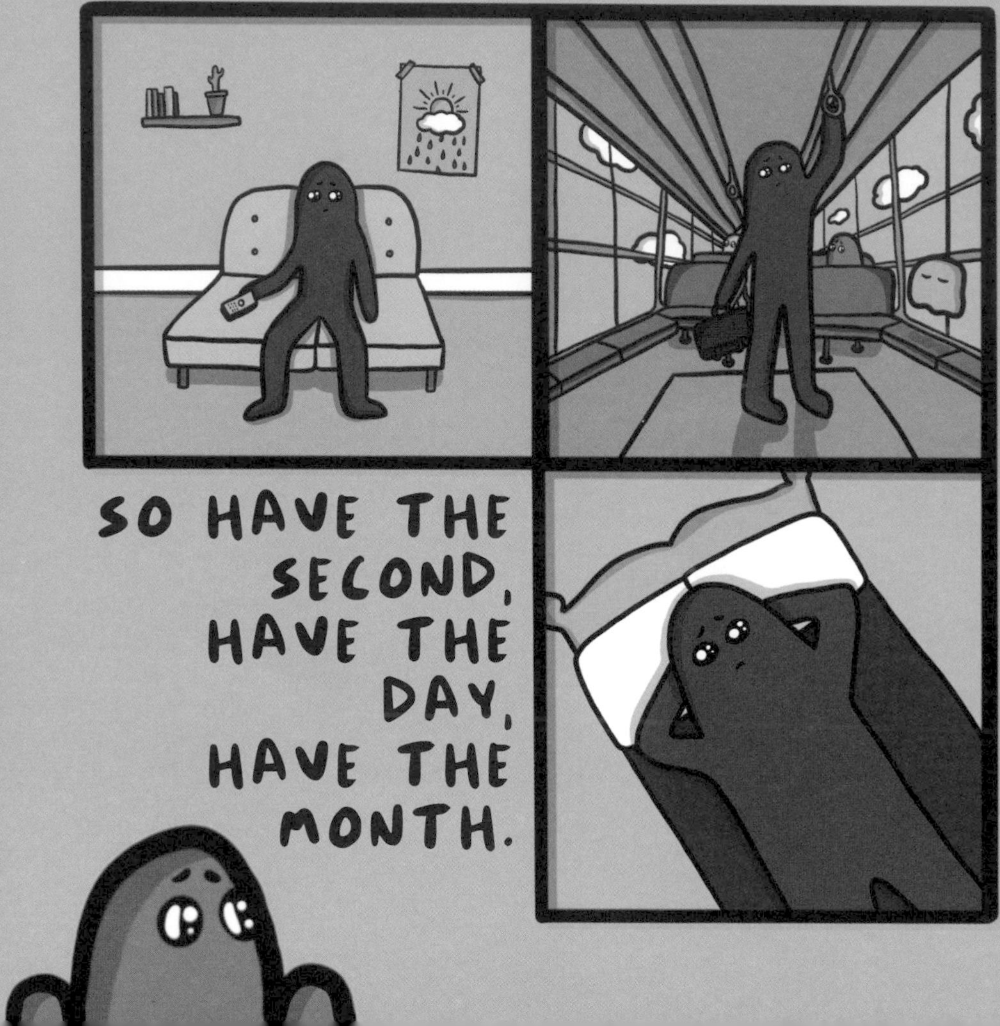
SO HAVE THE SECOND, HAVE THE DAY, HAVE THE MONTH.

BUT WE'RE NOT GOING TO LET IT HAVE OUR LIFE.

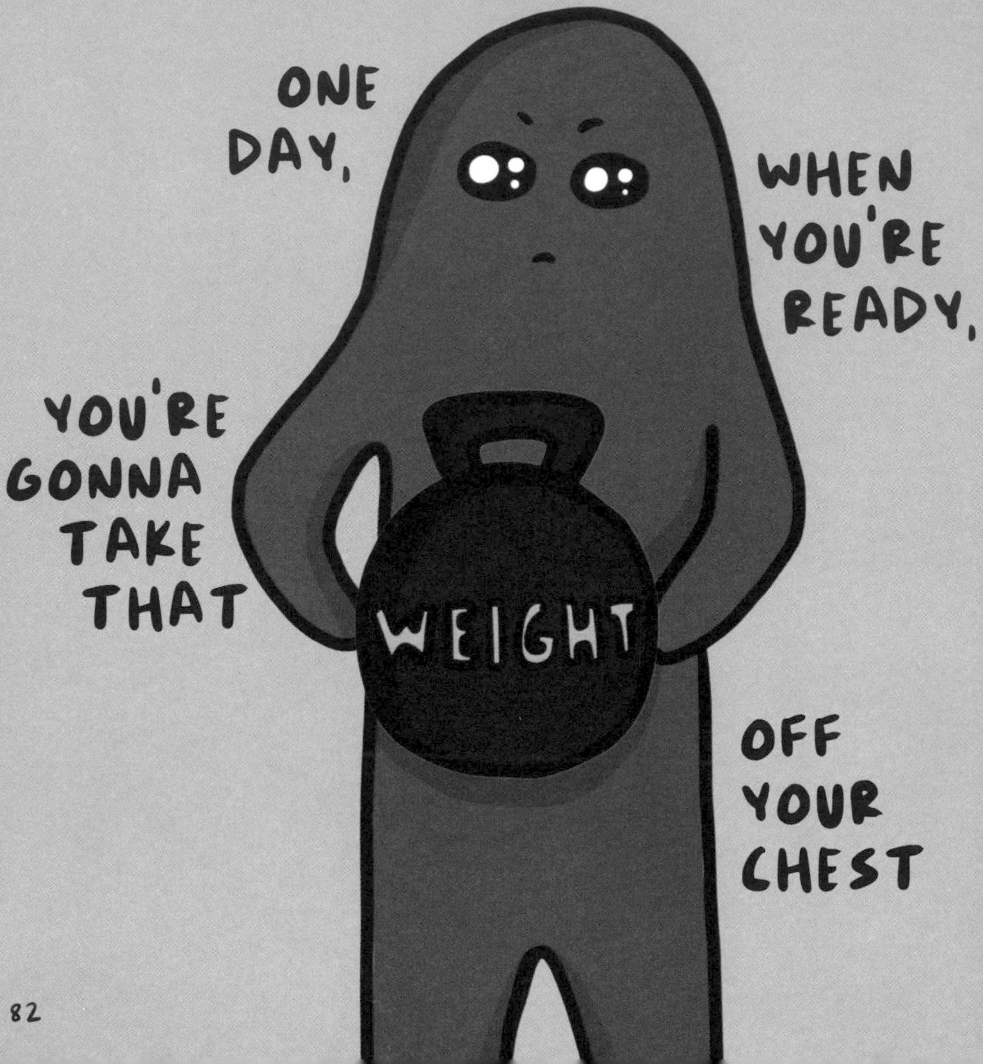
ONE DAY,
WHEN YOU'RE READY,
YOU'RE GONNA TAKE THAT
WEIGHT
OFF YOUR CHEST

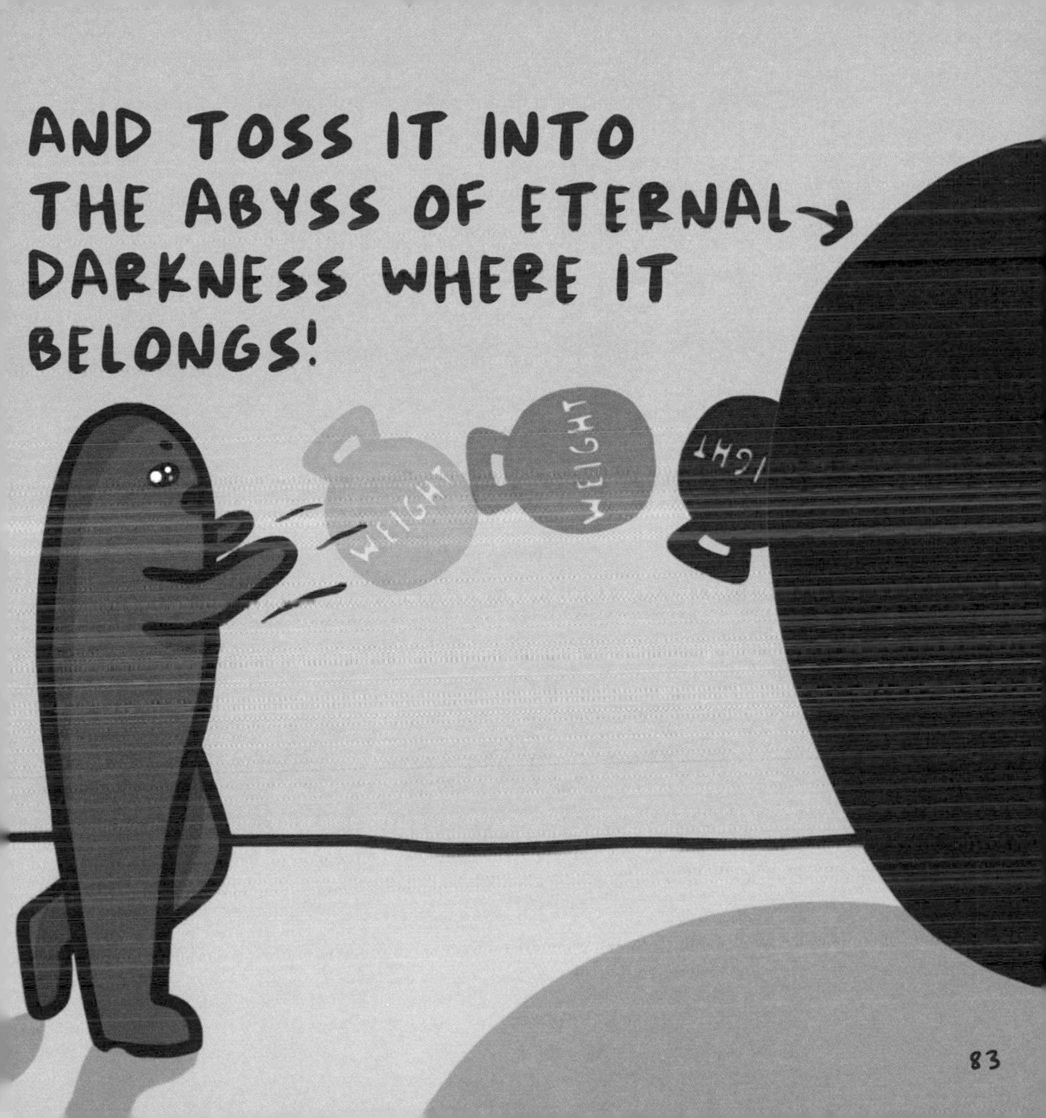
AND TOSS IT INTO THE ABYSS OF ETERNAL DARKNESS WHERE IT BELONGS!
WEIGHT
WEIGHT
IGHT

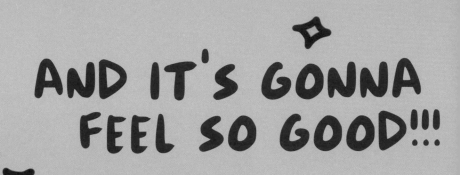

AND IT'S GONNA FEEL SO GOOD!!!

YOU DESERVE
TO FEEL

LIGHT,

AND

AIRY

AND

BREEZY,

LIKE
A
SOFT
LITTLE
SOUFFLE.

I BELIEVE IN YOU AND

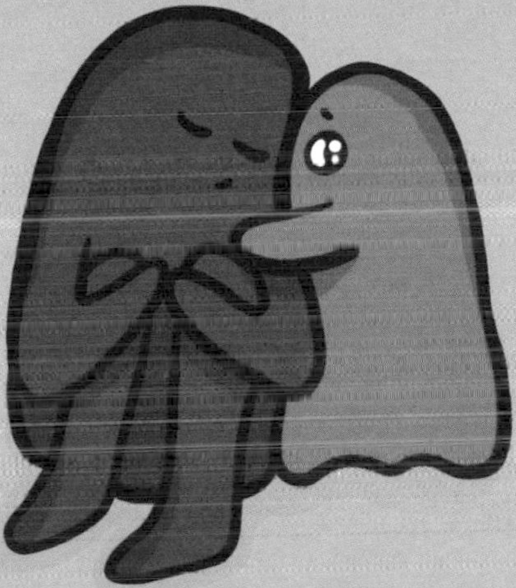

I LOVE YOU SO MUCH.

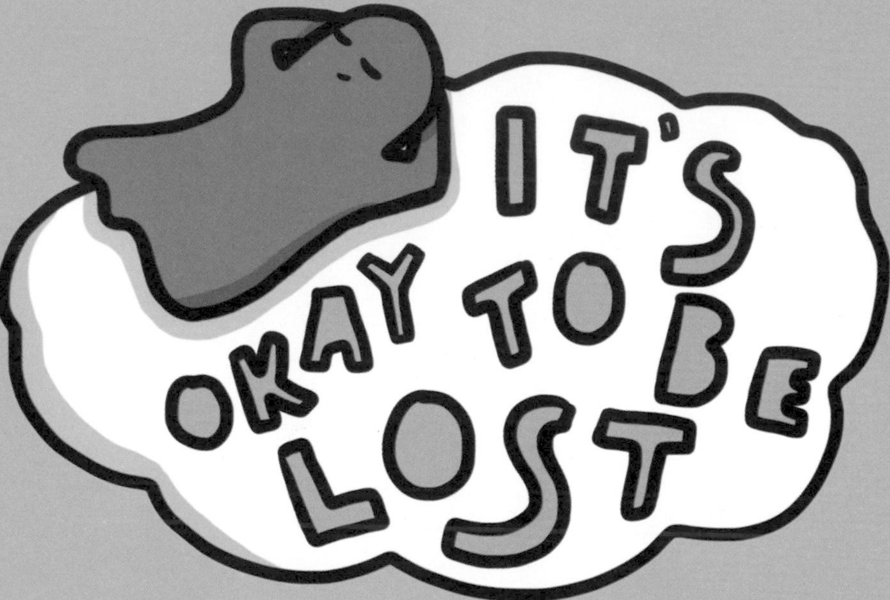
IT'S OKAY TO BE LOST

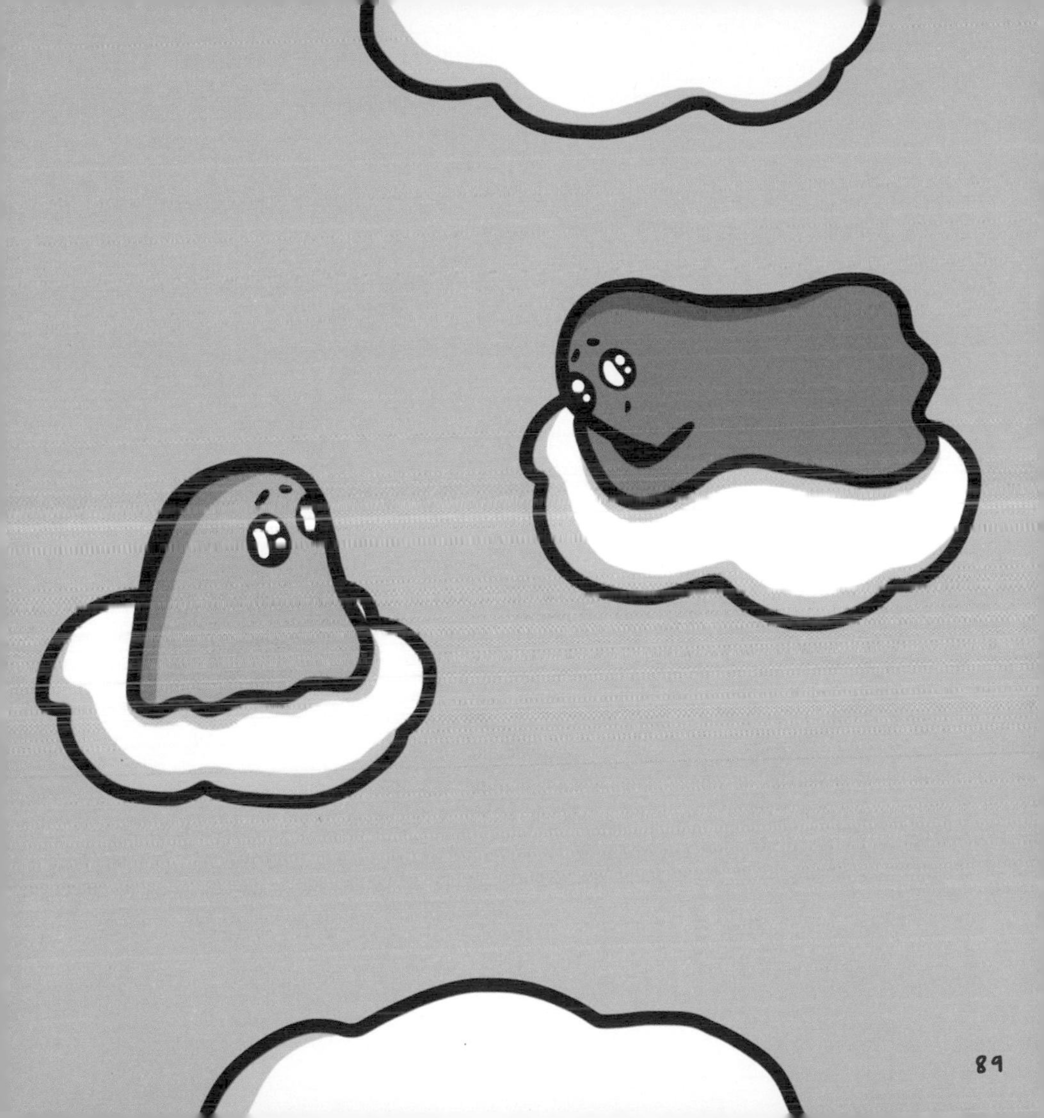

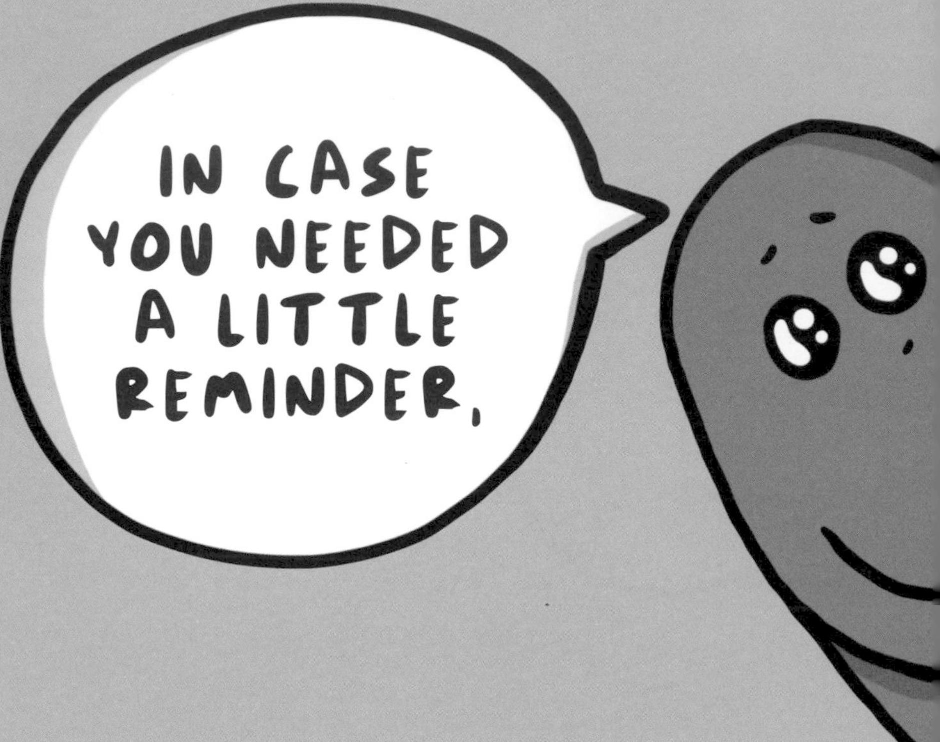
IN CASE YOU NEEDED A LITTLE REMINDER,

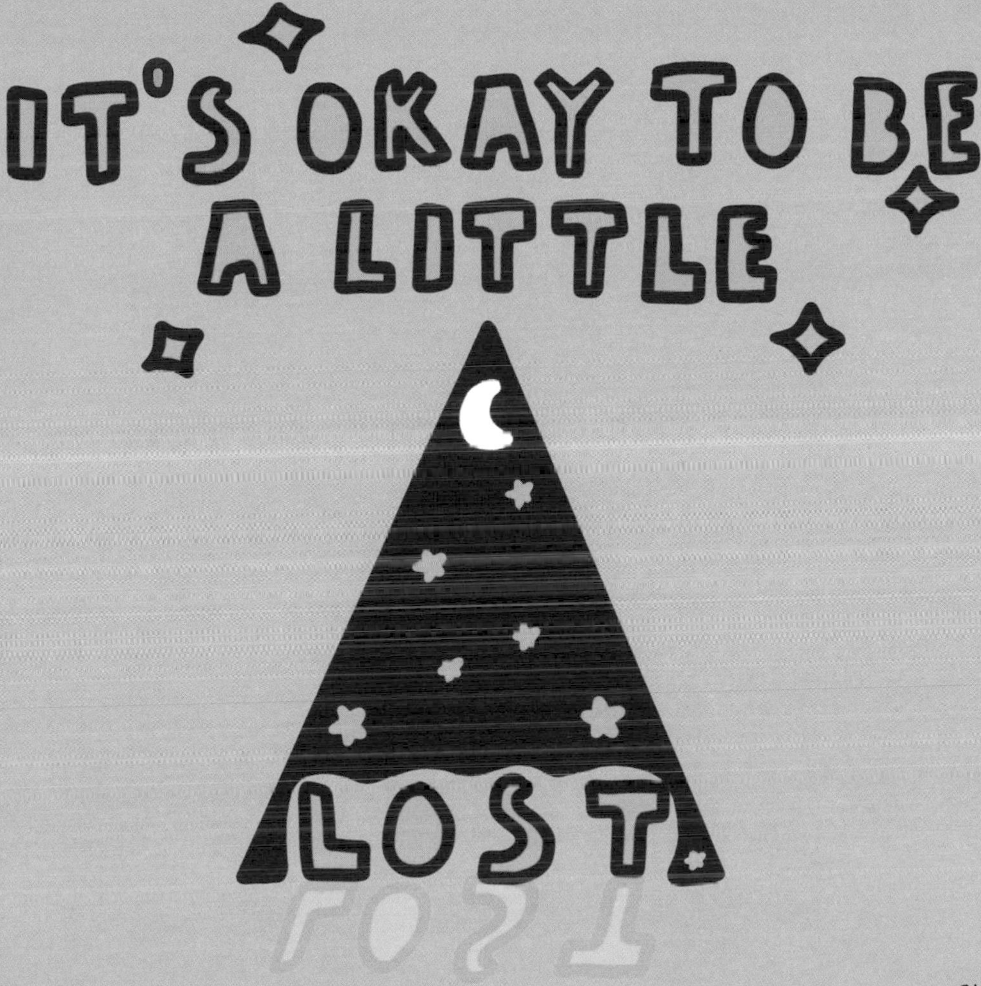
IT'S OKAY TO BE
A LITTLE
LOST

IF YOU WERE ALWAYS
IN COMPLETE CONTROL
OF EVERYTHING

24/7

LIFE WOULD BE

SO BORING!!

SO MY REQUEST FOR YOU IS TO REVEL IN THE

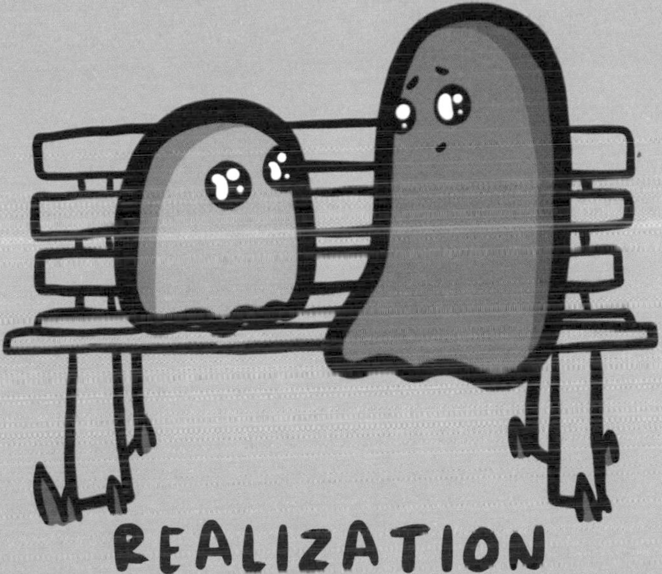

REALIZATION THAT BEING LOST IS KIND OF DOPE BECAUSE

what happens
next is the

FINDING.

YOU GET TO
FIND
A NEW

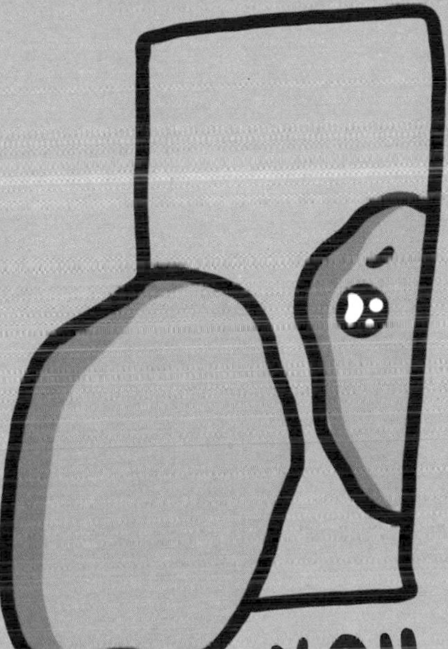

YOU.

A NEW

SOMEBODY
ELSE.

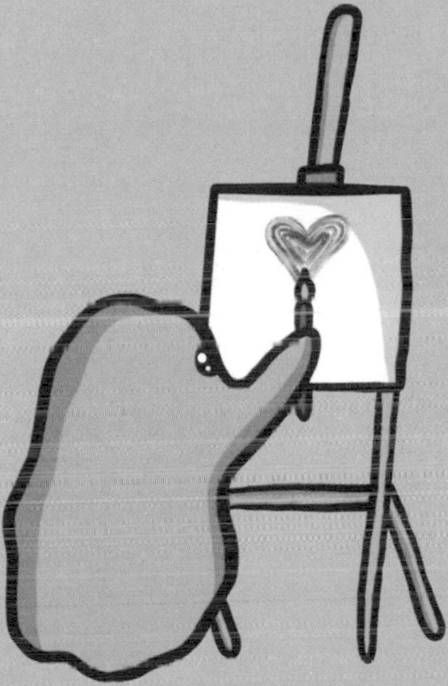

AS LONG AS YOU'RE SITTING IN YOUR LOST-NESS WITH A BIG OPEN HEART

THAT'S READY TO ACCEPT WHATEVER'S NEXT, THEN...

what's meant for you will NEVER miss you.

99

I'M SO EXCITED

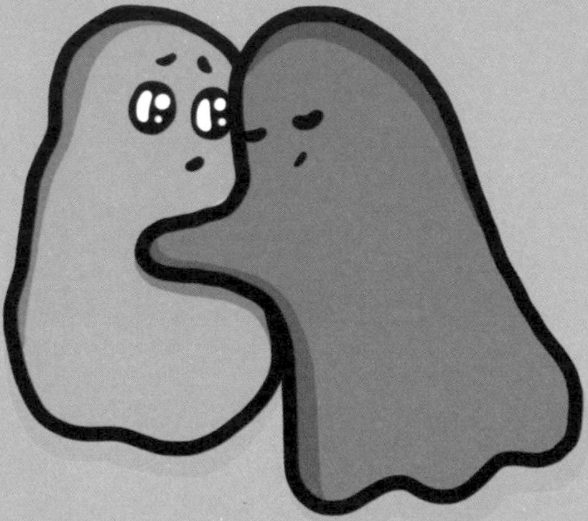

TO SEE WHAT YOU FIND.

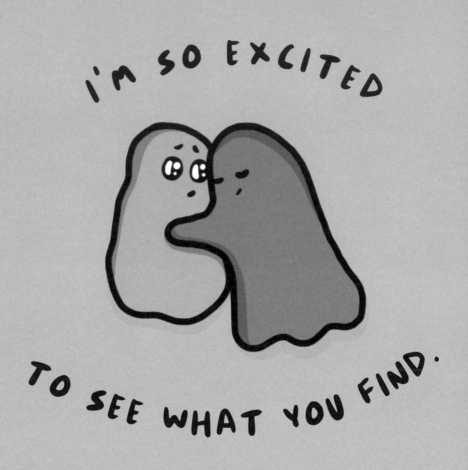

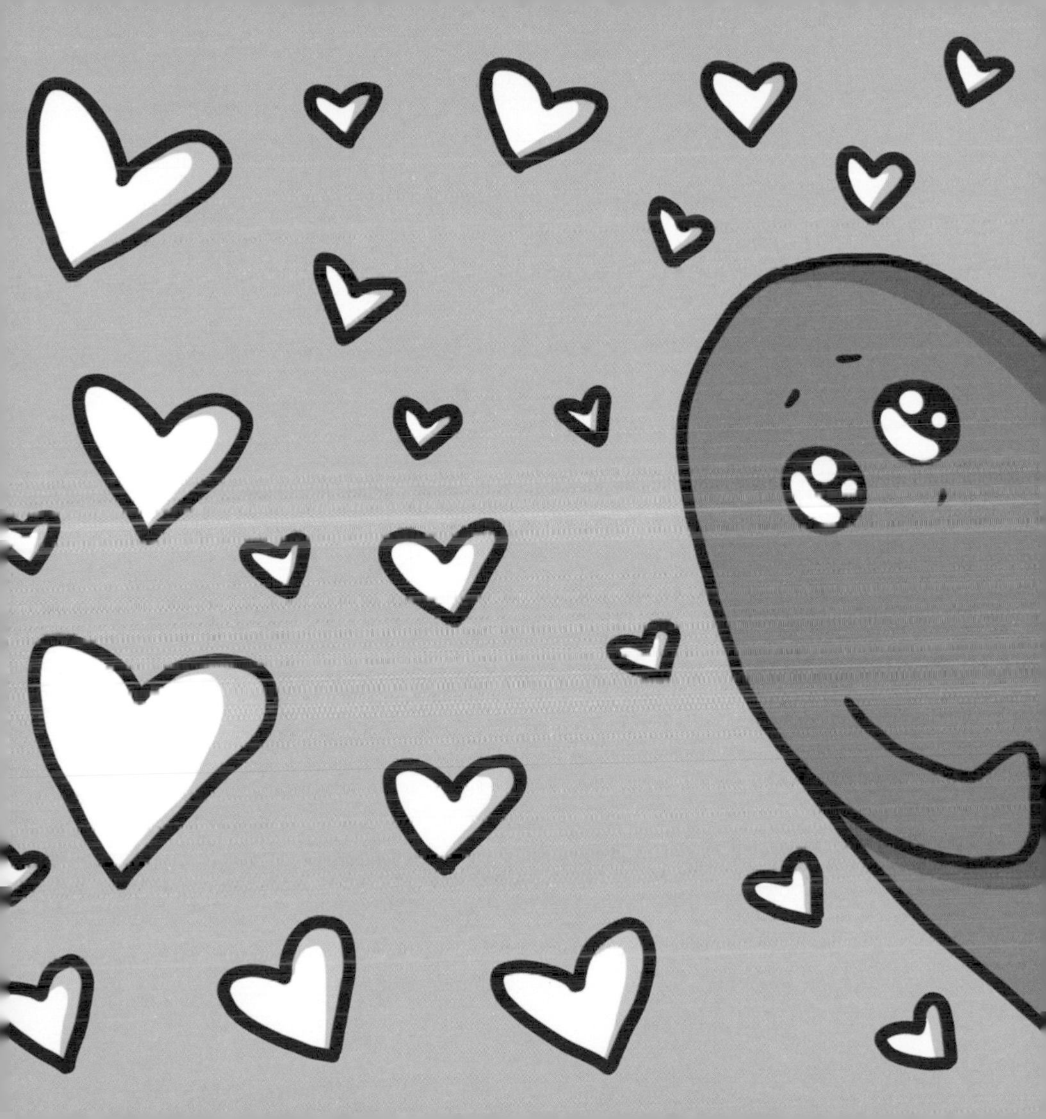

III

The Finding

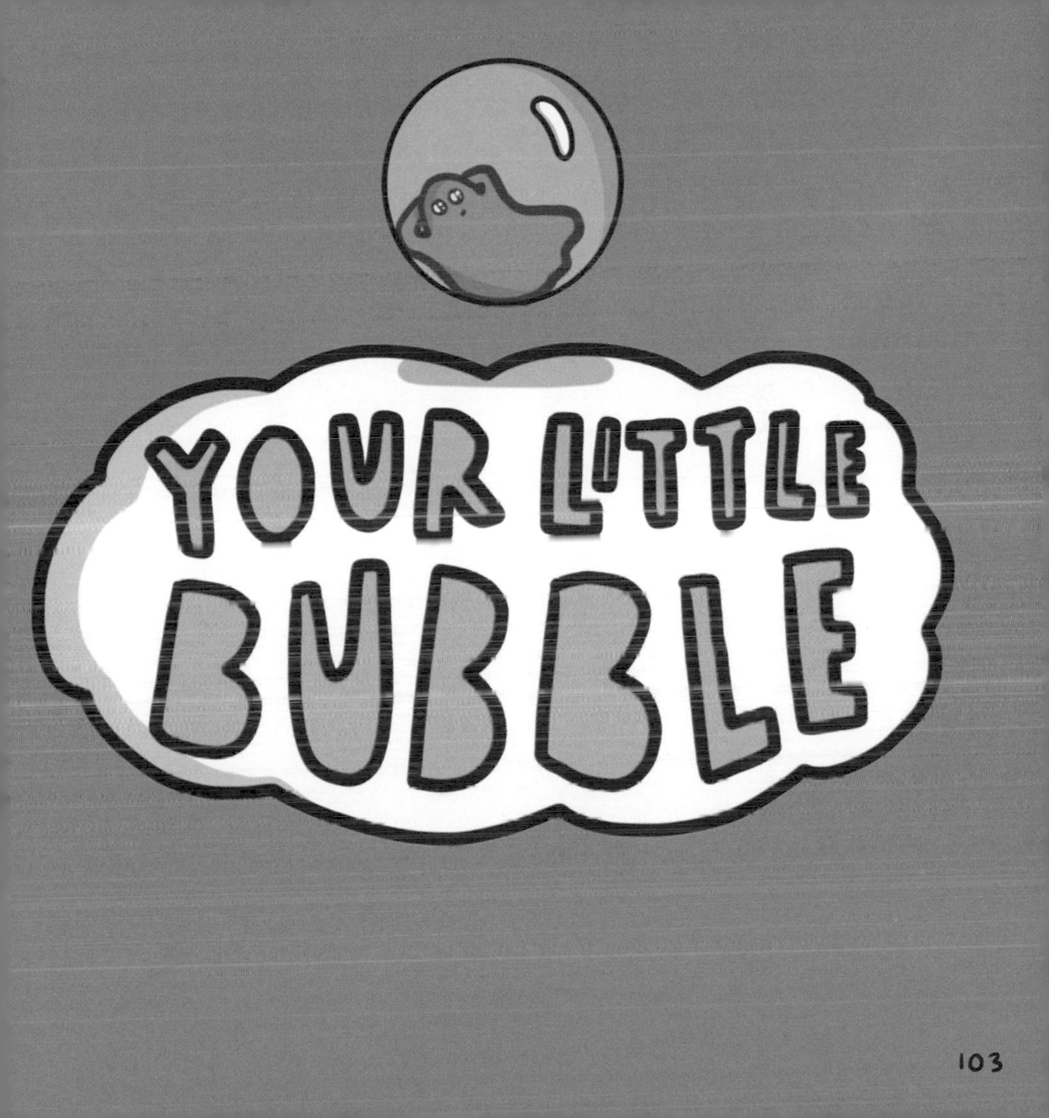

YOUR LITTLE BUBBLE

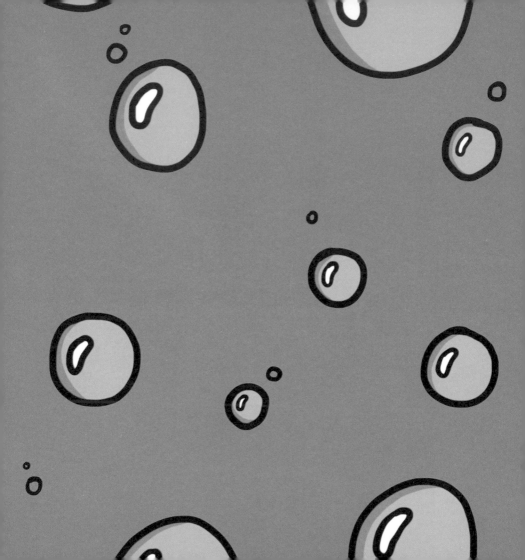

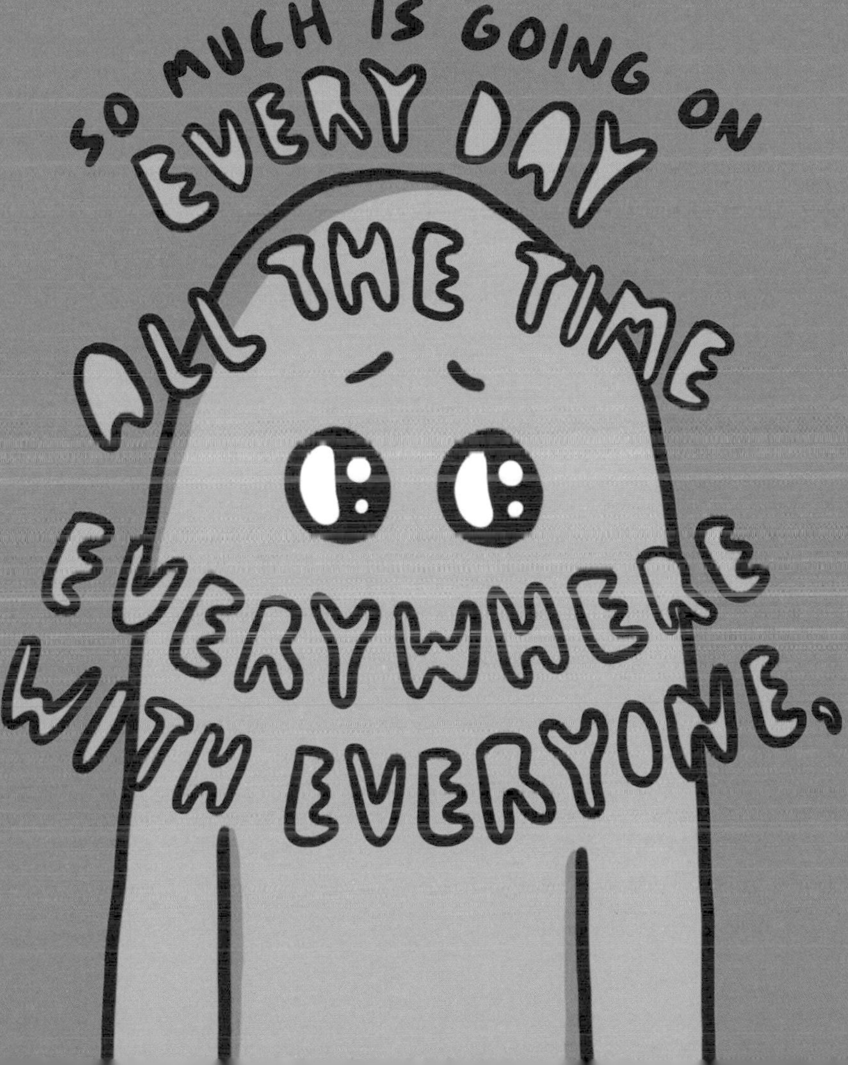
SO MUCH IS GOING ON
EVERY DAY
ALL THE TIME
EVERYWHERE
WITH EVERYONE.

AND IT'S SO EASY TO SEE

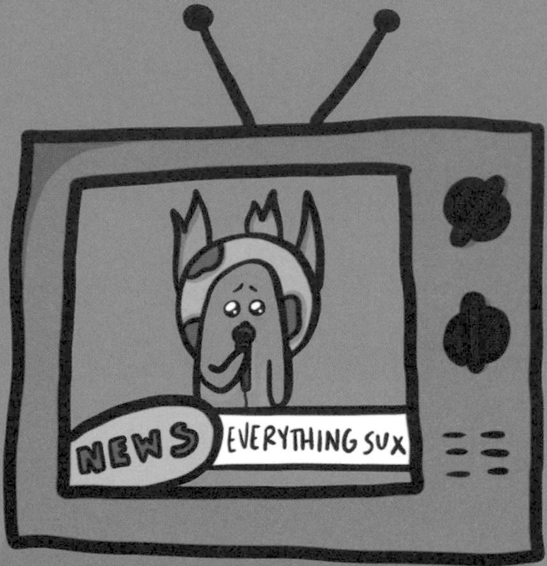
NEWS
EVERYTHING SUX

WHAT'S GOING
ON WITH THE WORLD.

AND WHAT'S GOING ON

WITH YOUR FRIENDS,

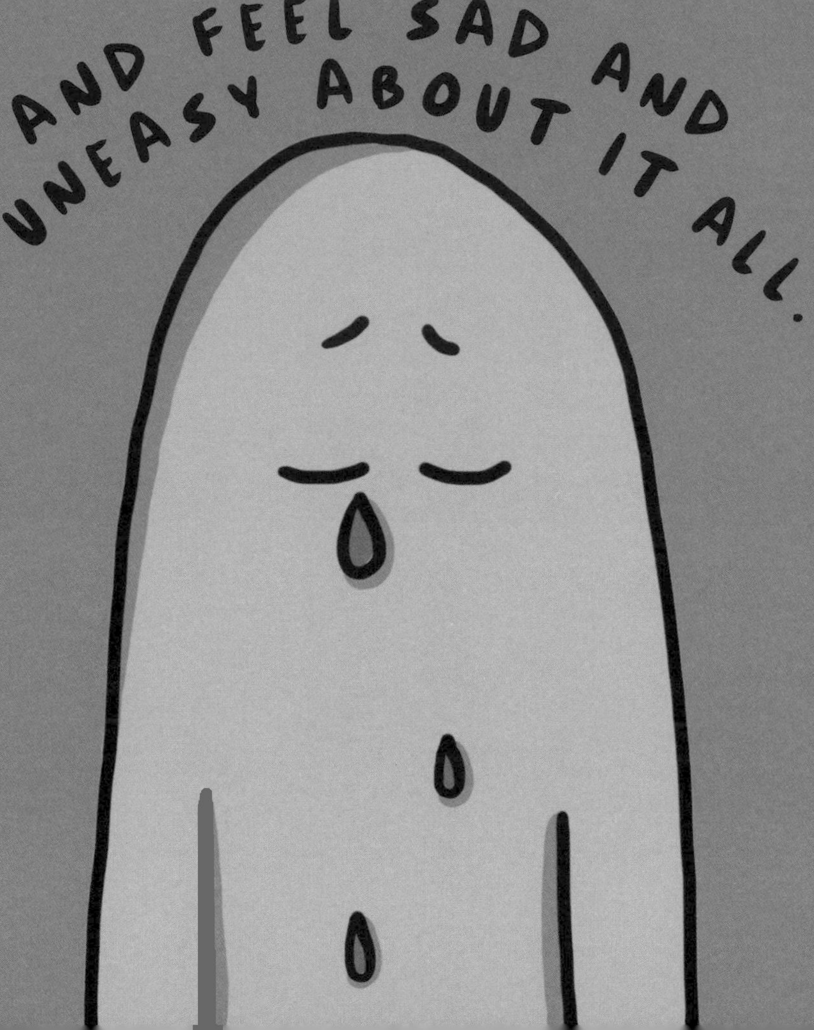
AND FEEL SAD AND
UNEASY ABOUT IT ALL.

AND THAT'S OKAY!

THAT MEANS YOU'RE A REAL HUMAN! WITH FEELINGS AND EMOTIONS! AND EMPATHY!

110

BUT
THIS IS YOUR
REMINDER
THAT

YOU'RE ALLOWED TO CRAWL BACK INTO THE SHELL OF YOU
AND STAY THERE FOR A MINUTE.

AND

BREATHE

AND

CHILL

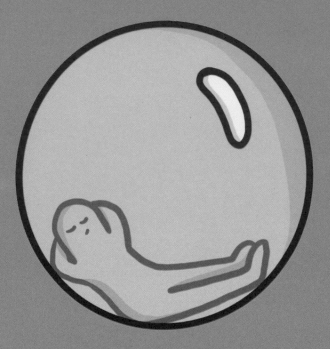

AND BE IN YOUR
LITTLE BUBBLE.

AND YOU CAN
LET EVERYTHING
BOUNCE OFF
UNTIL YOU FEEL
LIKE YOU WANNA
COME BACK OUT.

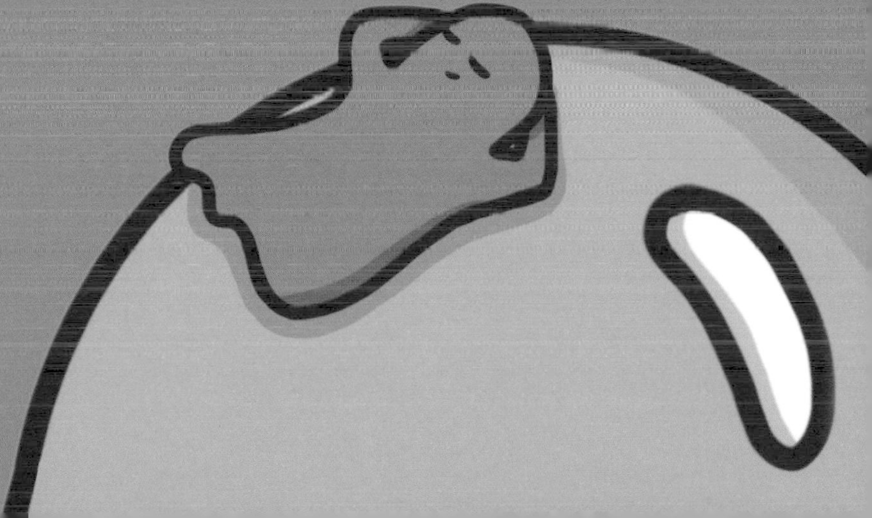

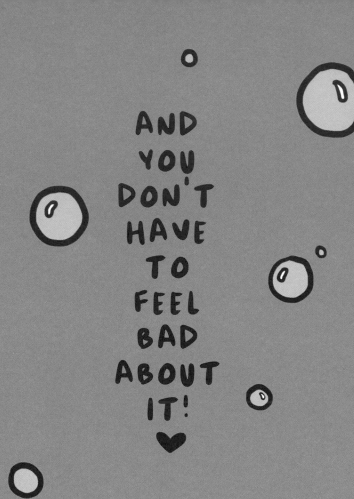

AND YOU DON'T HAVE TO FEEL BAD ABOUT IT! ♥

116

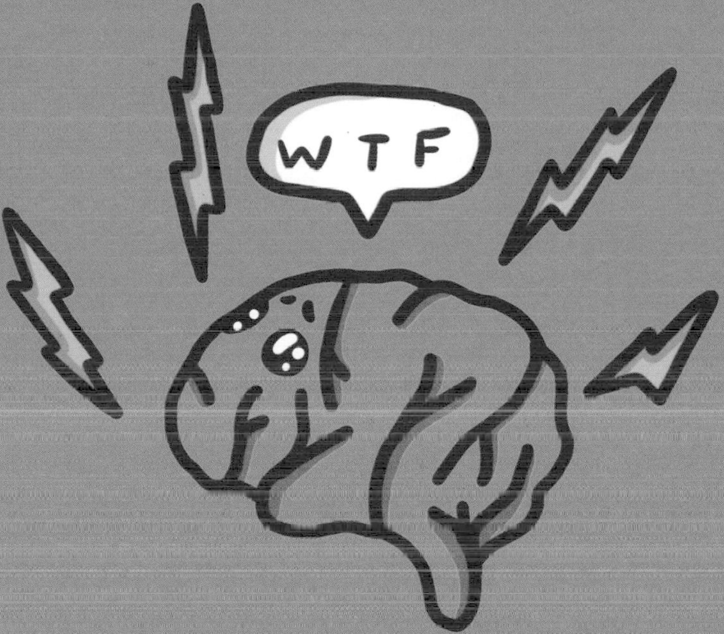
WTF

WE WERE NEVER MEANT TO HAVE SO MUCH BOMBARDING OUR BEAUTIFUL LITTLE BRAINS ALL THE TIME.

SO BE GENTLE WITH
YOURS BECAUSE

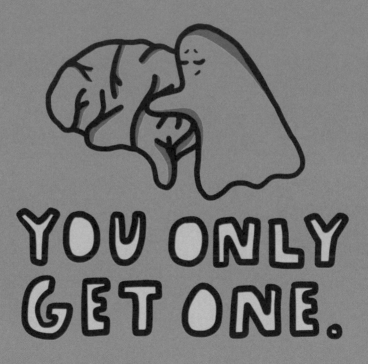

YOU ONLY
GET ONE.

CHOSEN FAMILY

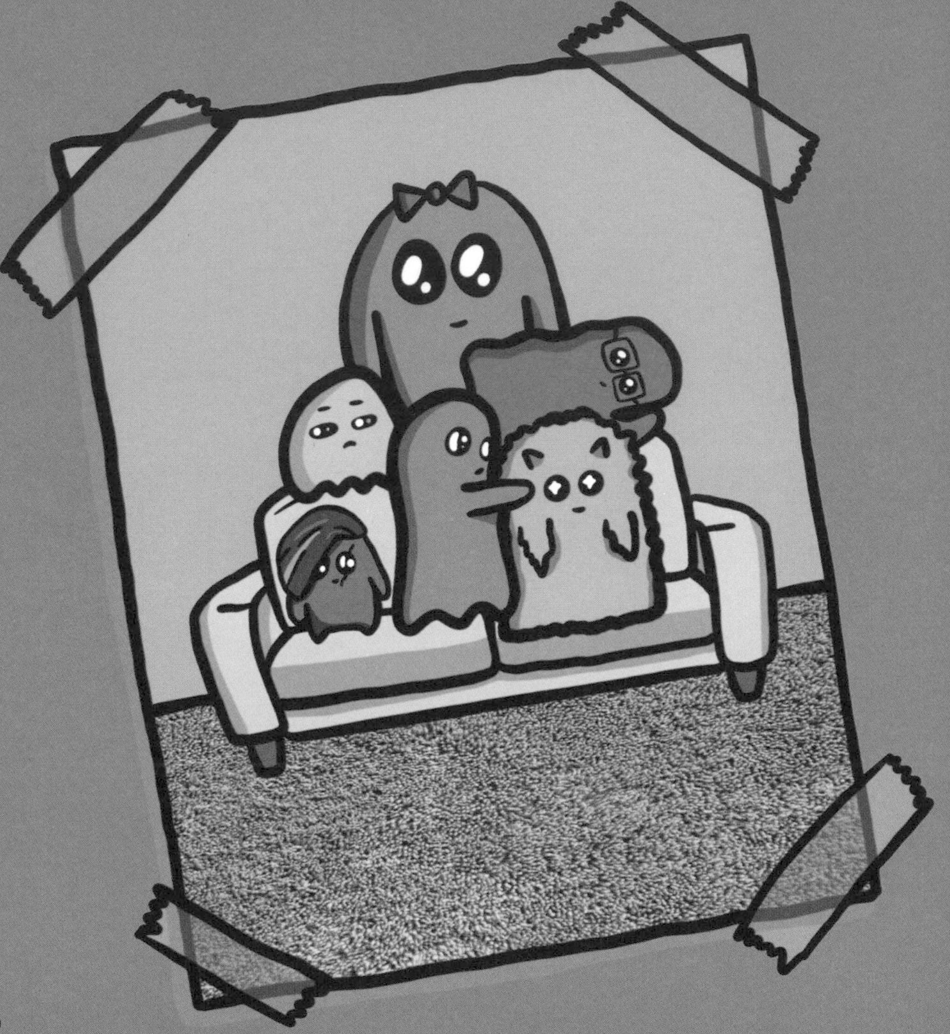

WE ALL HAVE A
FAMILY THAT WE'RE
BORN WITH...

AND SOMETIMES THAT
FAMILY LOOKS A LIL'
DIFFERENT FROM WHAT
YOU SEE

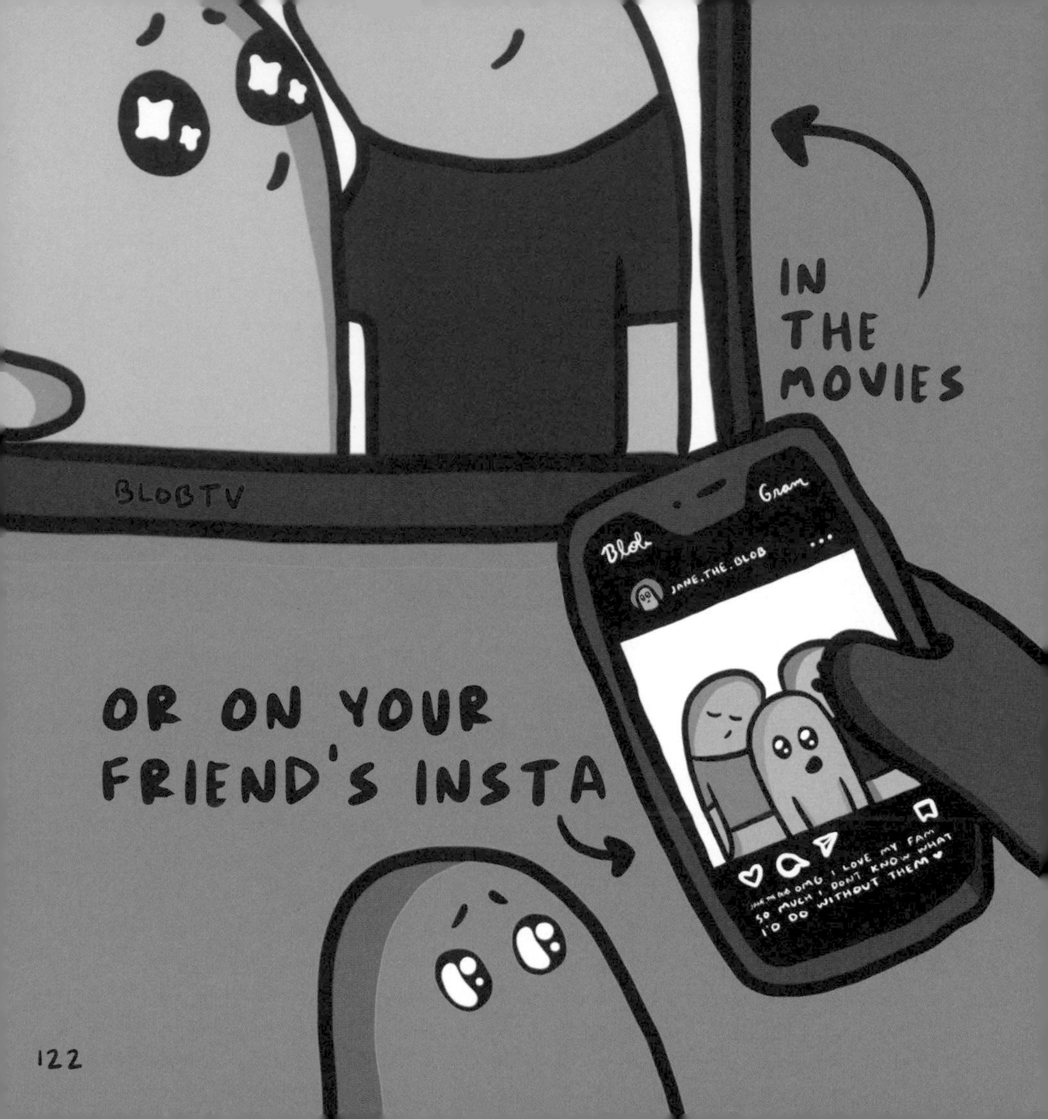
IN THE MOVIES
BLOBTV
Gram
Blob
JANE.THE.BLOB
OMG I LOVE MY FAM SO MUCH I DONT KNOW WHAT I'D DO WITHOUT THEM ♥
OR ON YOUR FRIEND'S INSTA

AND SOMETIMES THAT
FAMILY ISN'T EVEN

IN THE PICTURE
ANYMORE.

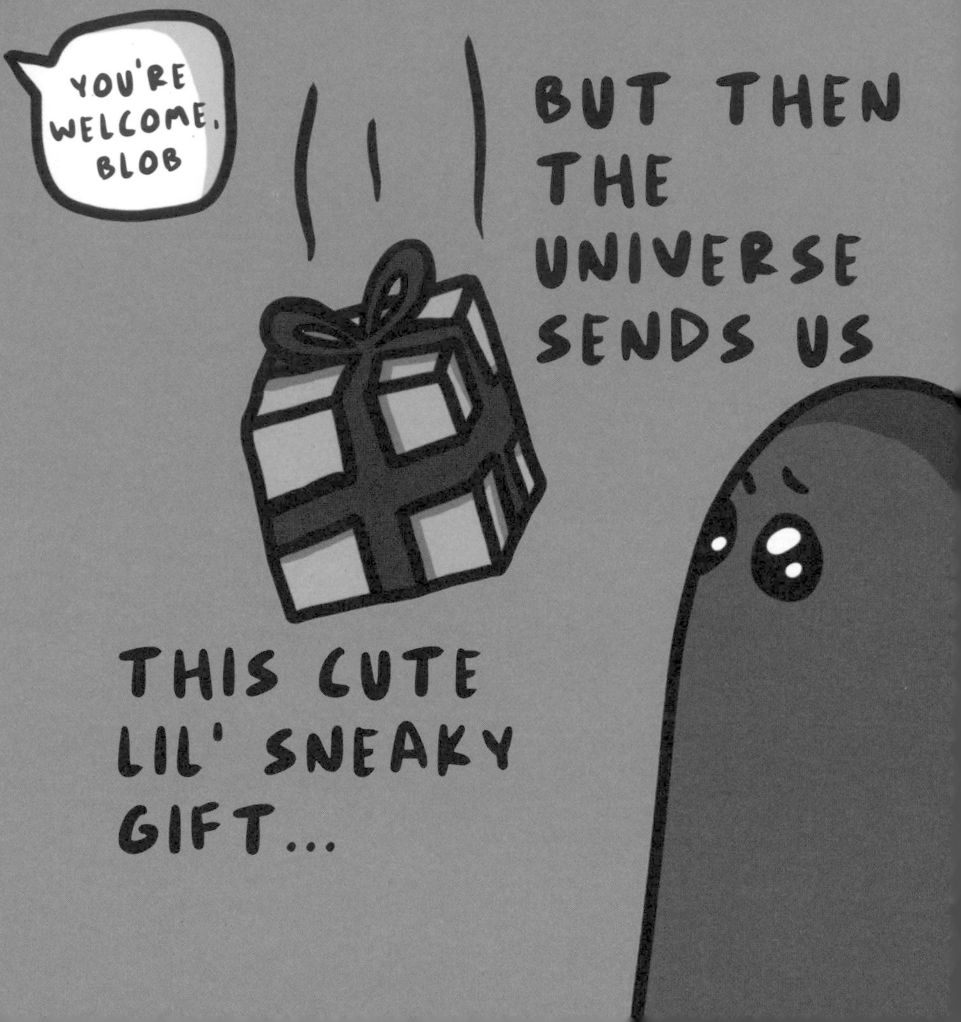
YOU'RE WELCOME, BLOB
BUT THEN THE UNIVERSE SENDS US
THIS CUTE LIL' SNEAKY GIFT...

A FAMILY,
THAT WE
CHOOSE

125

AND IT CAN BE ANYONE!

ANYONE WHO LOVES YOU AND IS THERE TO SUPPORT YOU

UNCONDITIONALLY.

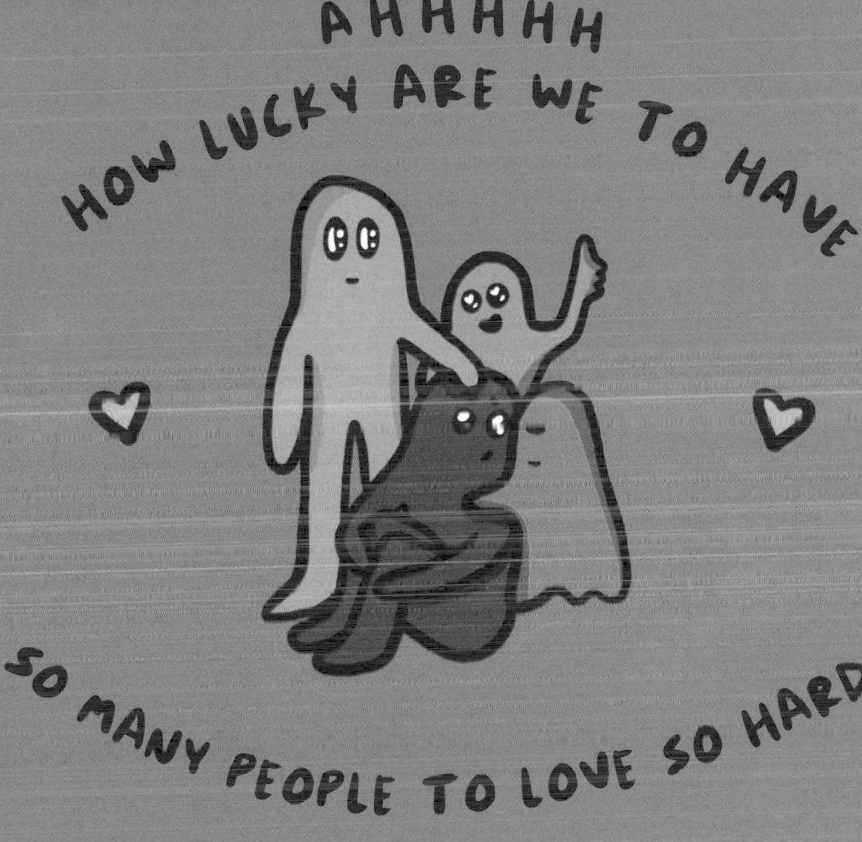
AHHHHH
HOW LUCKY ARE WE TO HAVE
SO MANY PEOPLE TO LOVE SO HARD?!

NO MATTER WHAT YOUR "FAMILY" LOOKS LIKE RIGHT NOW, BE SURE TO HUG 'EM A LITTLE TIGHTER.

YOU WON'T REGRET IT.

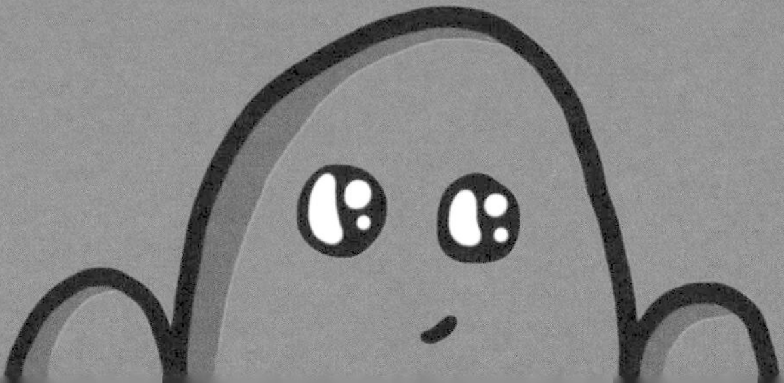

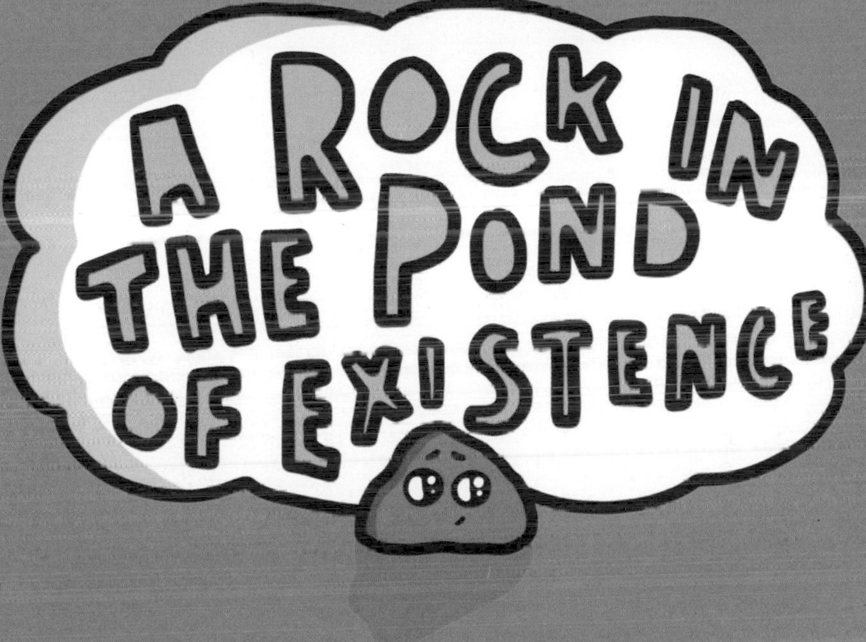
A ROCK IN THE POND OF EXISTENCE

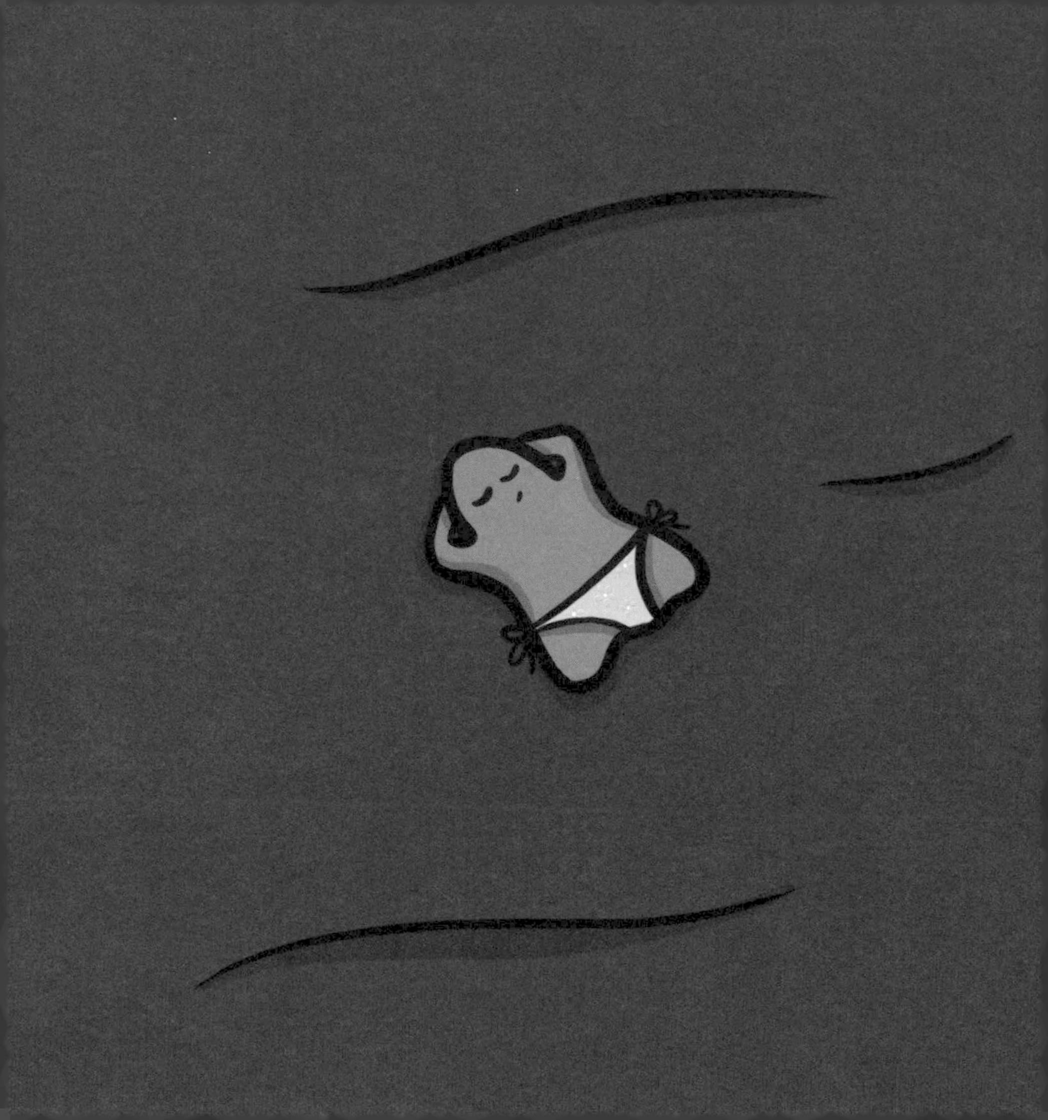

SOMETIMES I
STRUGGLE WITH
MY SENSE OF
PURPOSE.

131

I'M LIKE,

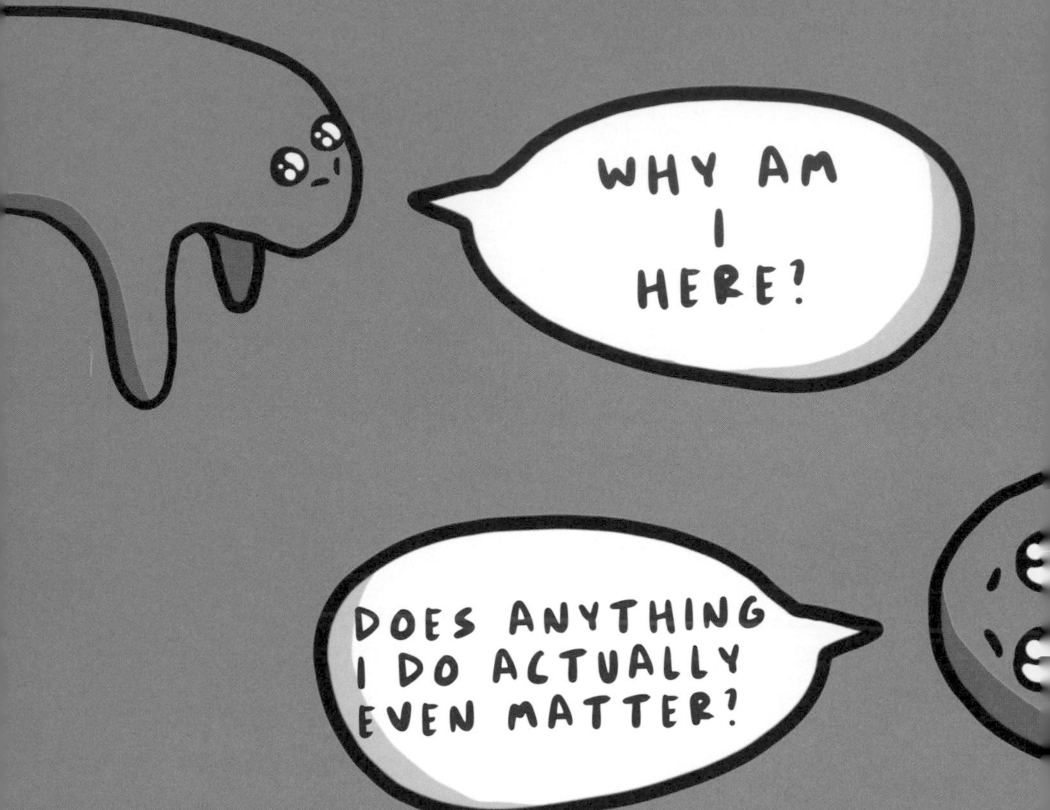
WHY AM I HERE?
DOES ANYTHING I DO ACTUALLY EVEN MATTER?

AND I WAS TRYNA
FIGURE IT OUT,
AND I WAS TRIPPIN'
ABOUT IT...

AND THEN I HAD THIS

BLOB
REVELATION

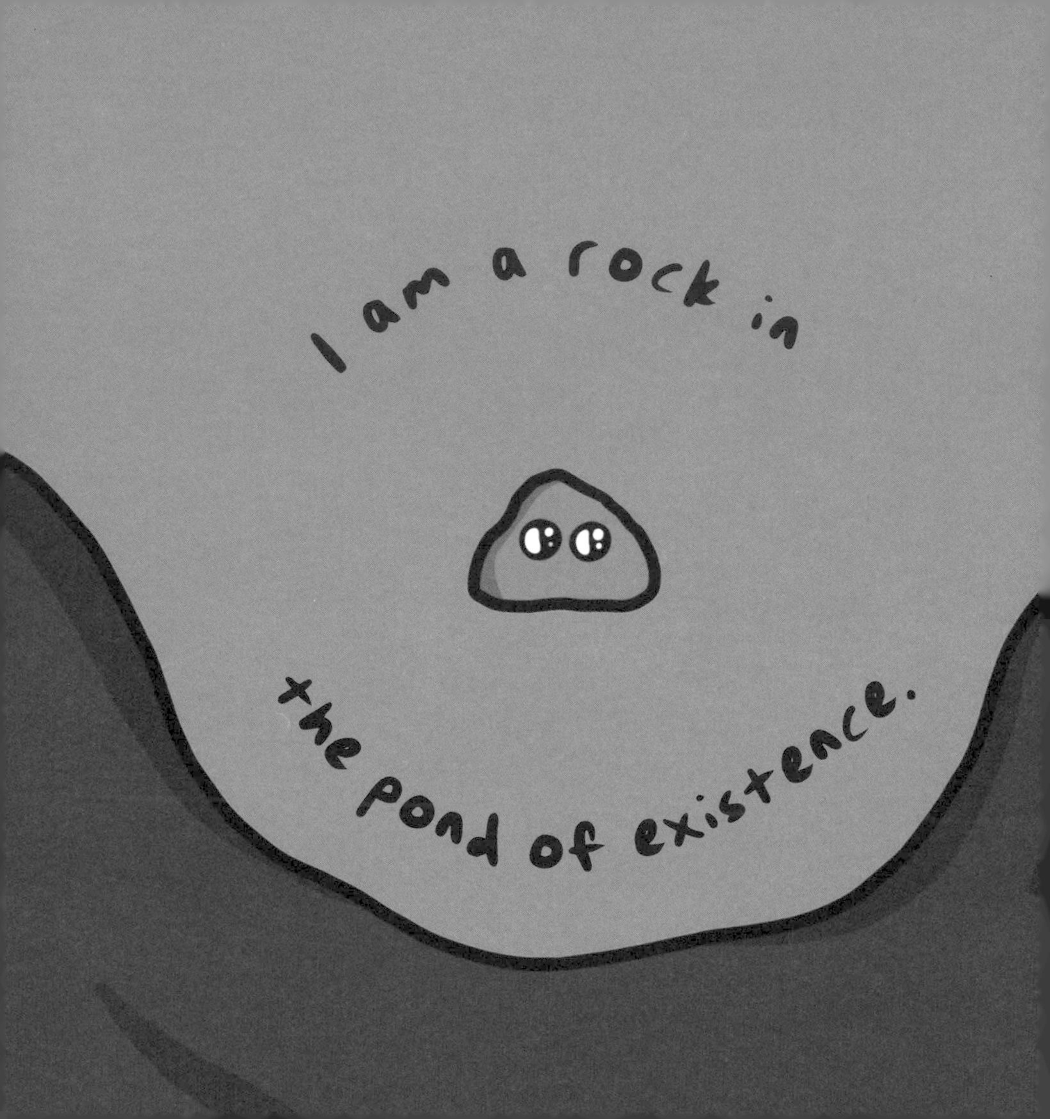
I am a rock in
the pond of existence.

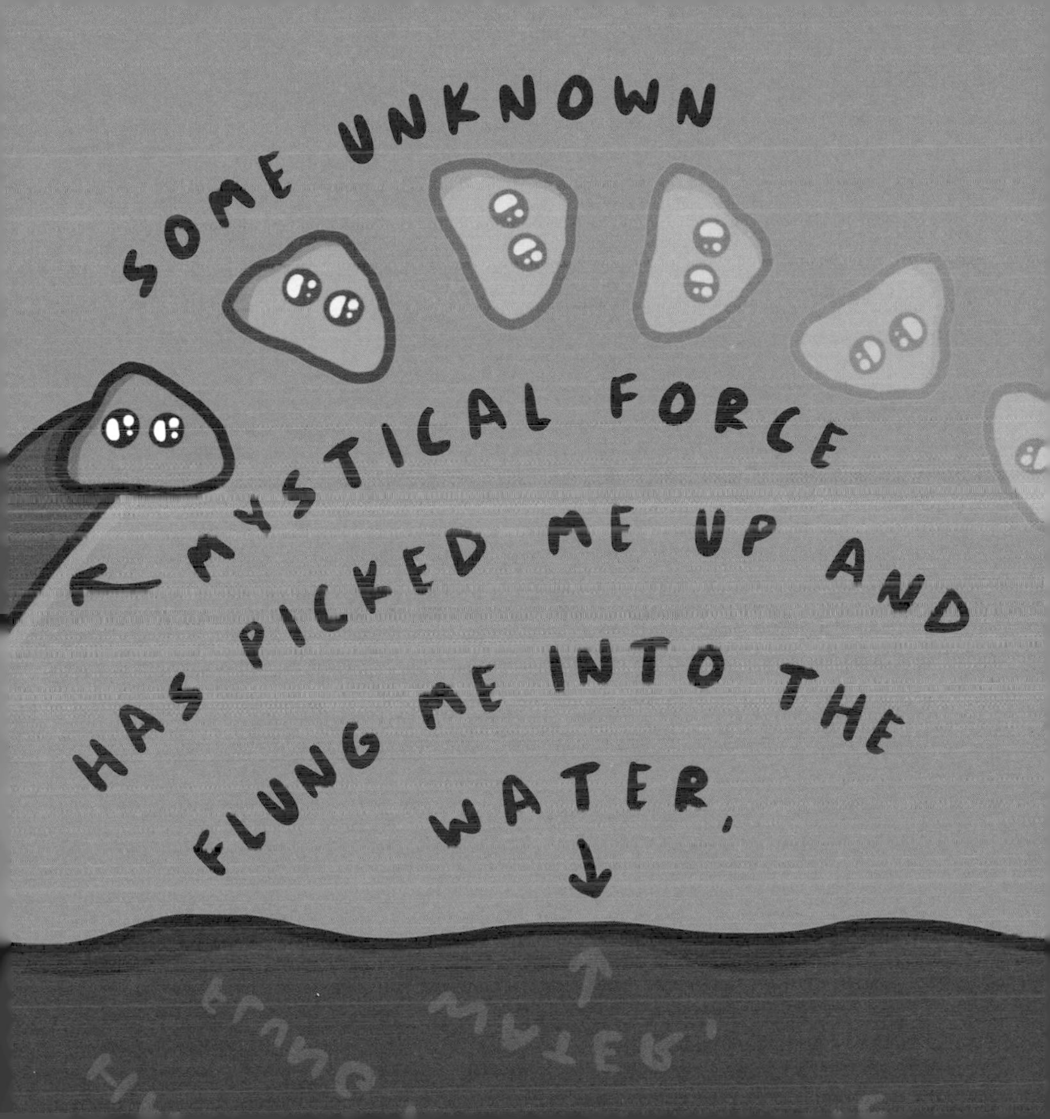
SOME UNKNOWN MYSTICAL FORCE HAS PICKED ME UP AND FLUNG ME INTO THE WATER,

AND I'M SPENDING
SO MUCH TIME
WORRYING ABOUT
HOW BIG MY
SPLASH IS GONNA BE

THAT I FORGOT TO
LOOK AROUND

AND BE LIKE,

WOAH.

I AM A ROCK

THAT IS FLYING THROUGH THE AIR.

A **LITERAL!**

FLYING!

ROCK!

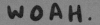

THERE WERE A TRILLION OTHER ROCKS THAT COULD HAVE BEEN PICKED UP AND TOSSED INTO THIS WEIRD ANOMALY OF AN EXPERIENCE.

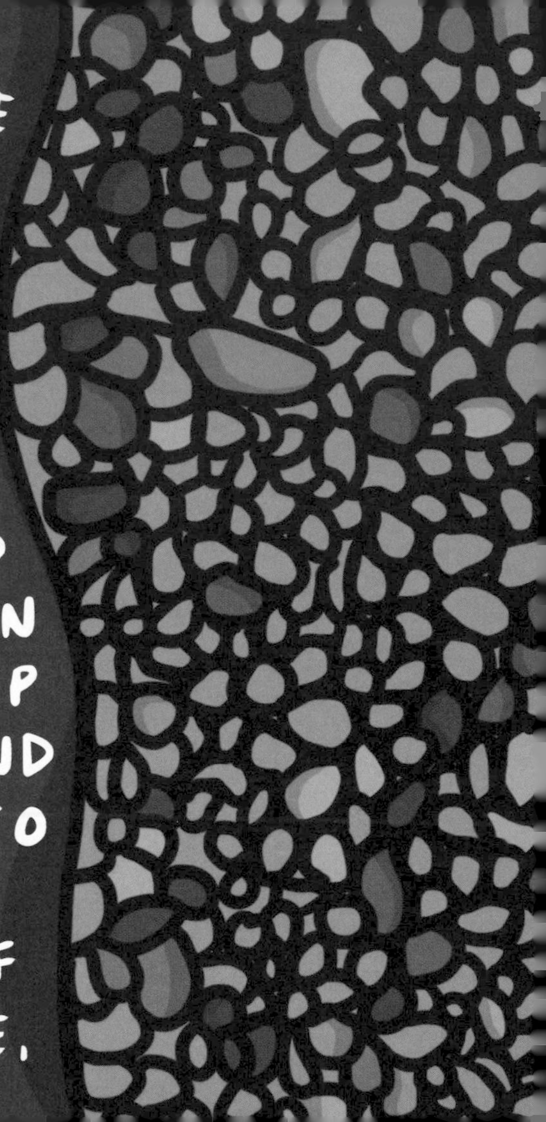

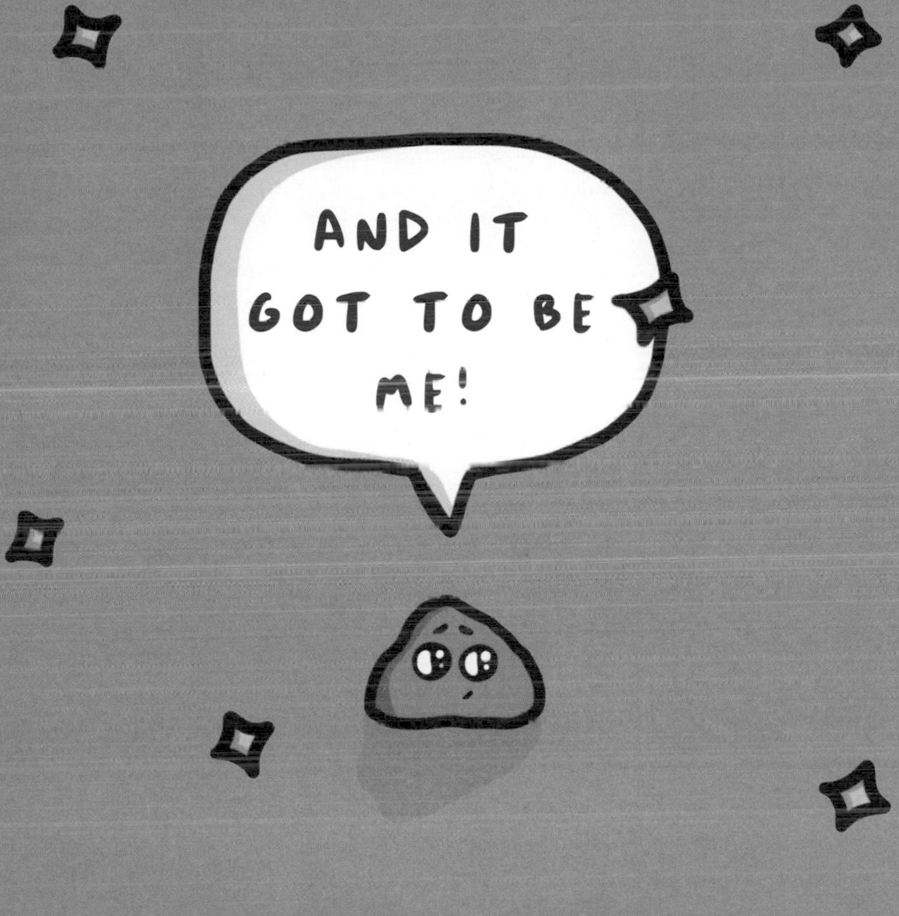
AND IT GOT TO BE ME!

I GUESS WHAT I'M
TRYNA SAY IS THAT
THE WORLD IS
TOO GOOD
AT MAKING US
BELIEVE THAT
WE HAVE TO

DO MORE
+
BE MORE
+
WANT MORE
+
HAVE MORE
WHEN

THE BEAUTY ISN'T IN THE PURPOSE,

IT'S IN THE PROCESS.

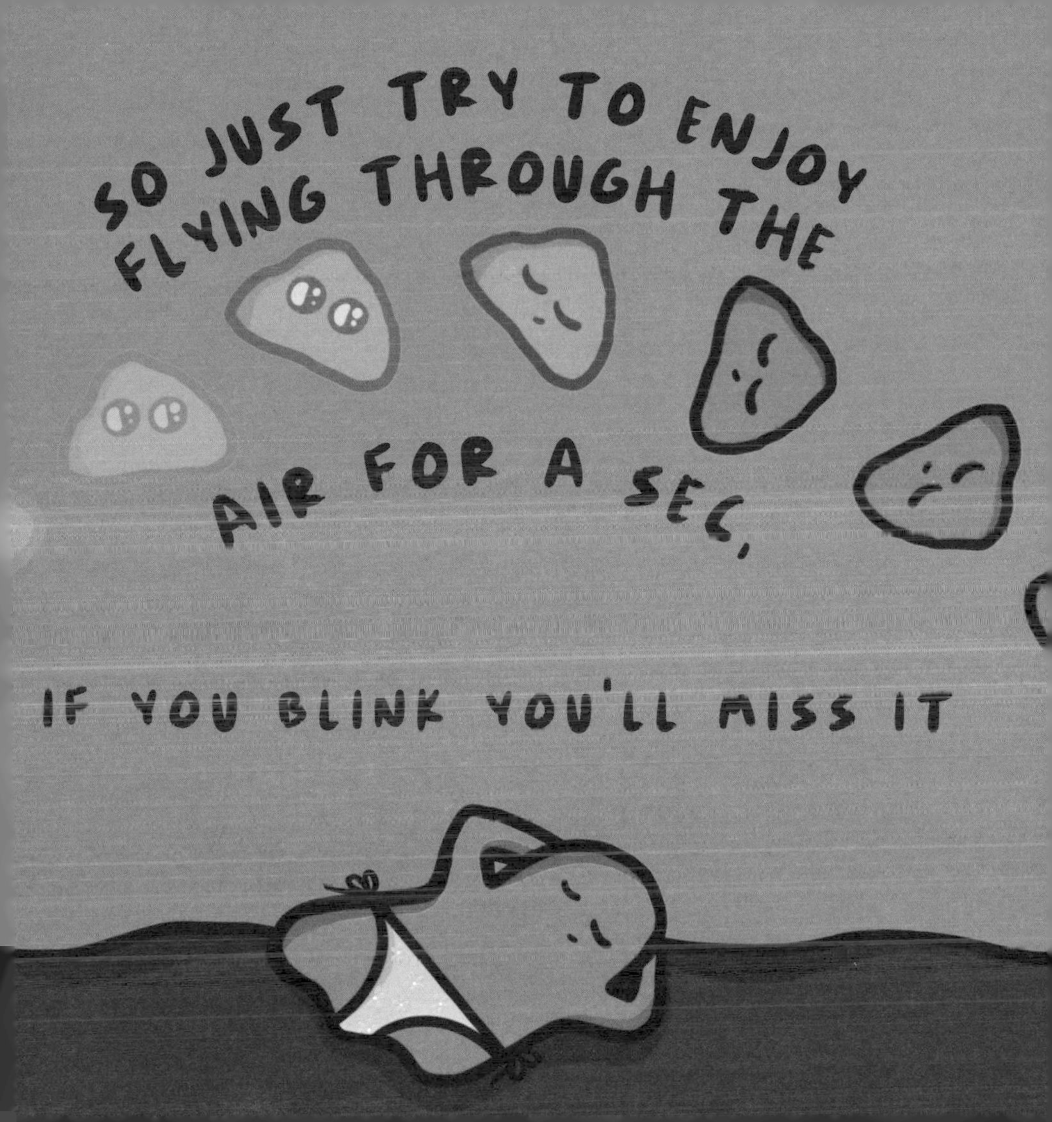
SO JUST TRY TO ENJOY
FLYING THROUGH THE
AIR FOR A SEC,
IF YOU BLINK YOU'LL MISS IT

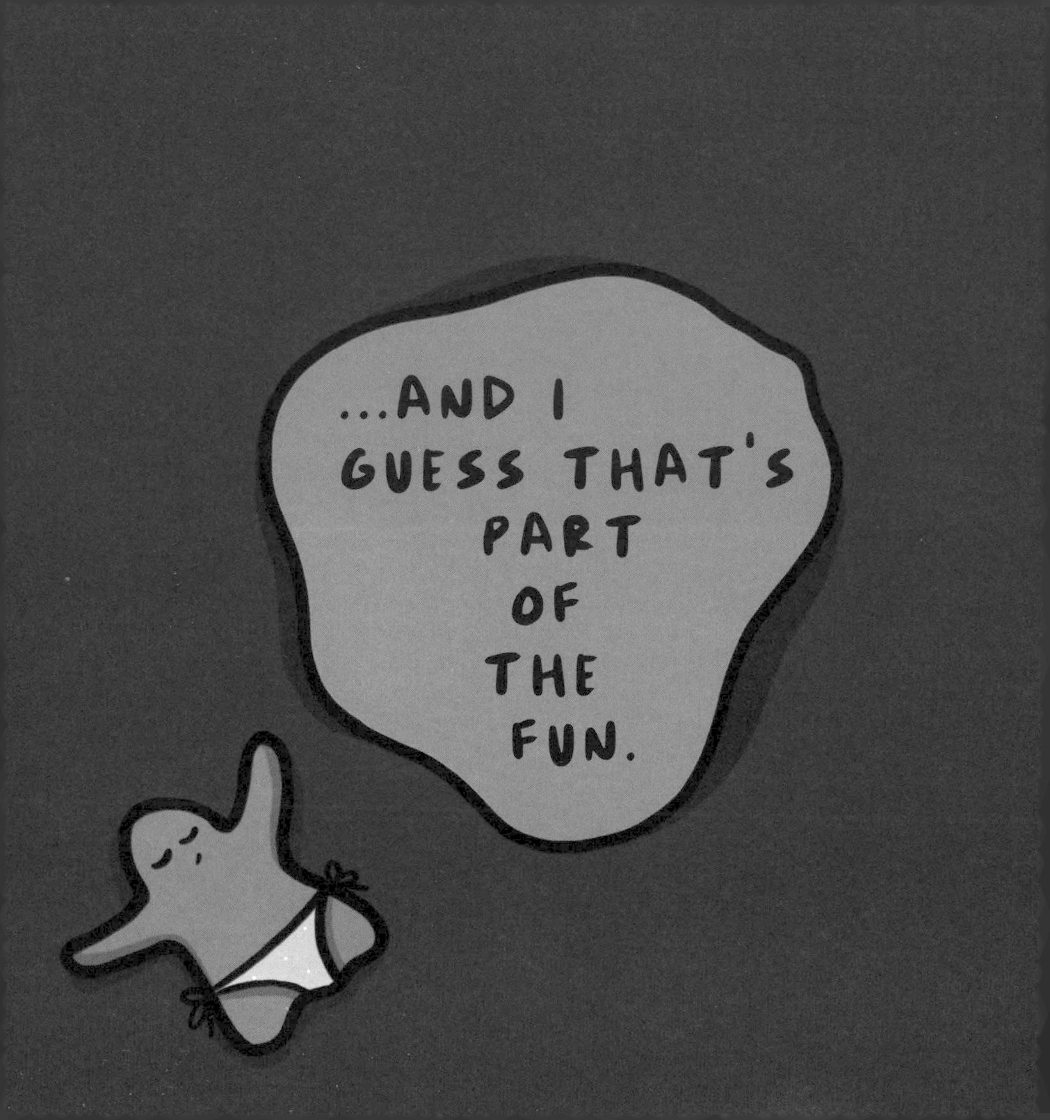
...AND I GUESS THAT'S PART OF THE FUN.